Operative Surgery

Viva Practice for the MRCS/AFRCS

Other Examination Preparation Books Published by Petroc Press:

Obtainable from all good booksellers or, in case of difficulty, from Plymbridge Distributors Limited, Plymbridge House, Estover Road, PLYMOUTH, Devon PL6 7PZ. Tel. 01752–202300; FAX 01752–202333

Operative Surgery
Viva Practice for the MRCS/AFRCS

K. M. Mokbel MB BS(London), FRCS(Eng), FRCS(Gen)

Consultant Surgeon
Academic Department of Breast Surgery
St. George's Hospital
London

T. A. Jeswani BSc(Hon.), MB BS(Hon.), MRCS(Ed)

Senior House Officer
Department of Surgery
St. George's Hospital
London

SECOND EDITION REVISED

 PETROC PRESS

Petroc Press, an imprint of LibraPharm Limited

Distributors
Plymbridge Distributors Limited, Plymbridge House, Estover Road, Plymouth
PL6 7PZ, UK

Original edition published under the title *Operative Surgery and Surgical Topics
for the FRCS* © Kluwer Academic Publishers, 1995

Revised edition published under the title *Operative Surgery and Surgical Topics
for the FRCS/MRCS* © LibraPharm Limited 1996

Second edition © LibraPharm Limited 1999
Second edition revised © LibraPharm Limited 2003

Published in the United Kingdom by
LibraPharm Limited
Gemini House
162 Craven Road
Newbury
Berkshire
RG14 5NR

A catalogue record for this book is available from the British Library

ISBN 1 900603 62 4

Printed and bound in the United Kingdom by
Cromwell Press, White Horse Business Park, Trowbridge, Wilts BA14 0XB

I dedicate this edition to my wife Hanadi and my son Leon.

K. M. Mokbel

Dedicated with love to my family and Katie.

T. A. Jeswani

Contents

Introduction

The viva (oral) part of postgraduate examinations in surgery has come to stay. It is no longer regarded as a final handshake for those who passed the clinical and written sections of the examinations. Indeed, a poor performance in the viva results in failure at the first hurdle of the new MRCS Part II examination. In the viva the examiners have the opportunity to assess:

1. the candidate's ability to communicate with professional colleagues;
2. the candidate's ability to comprehend the questions asked, analyse them and answer them logically;
3. the candidate's ability to make safe clinical decisions; and
4. the candidate's honesty and professional bearing.

This book provides an ideal revision guide for those preparing for the oral examination in operative surgery. It covers common general surgical operations and other topics loved by examiners such as screening, audit, medical statistics, trauma, life-saving procedures, controlled clinical trials and common postoperative complications. The various laparoscopic operations and recent advances in surgery have also been described. This book is best used with the help of a colleague who can play the role of the examiner.

Although this book has been written primarily for the MRCS (or FRCS) examination in the UK, it is undoubtedly valuable for candidates preparing for the certifying examinations of the American Board of General Surgery in the USA, the Australian Fellowship and the Canadian Board examinations.

Tips on Passing the Viva

1. Dress smartly but conservatively: avoid casual jackets, loud suits, loud ties, short skirts, etc.
2. Make sure that your hair is tidy and that you are clean shaven.
3. Appear confident and look the examiner in the eye.
4. Use concise, clear and simple English, in an audible voice.
5. Do not antagonise the examiners!
6. In the operative viva, when you are asked to describe an operation try to use the following methodical system (unless you are asked by the examiner to omit certain steps):
   - Preoperative preparation, e.g. informed consent, heparinisation for femoral embolectomy; bowel preparation for bowel surgery; premedication
   - Anaesthetic, local or general
   - Positioning the patient on the table
   - Skin cleansing and drapes
   - Incision
   - Initial assessment of findings
   - Procedure (including recognised difficulties and hazards)
   - Closure
   - Drains (if required)
   - Postoperative care (including treatment, investigations and nursing care)

SECTION 1

Applied Anatomy and Operative Surgery

Instruments and Sutures

Q1
How do you classify Vicryl sutures?

A1
Vicryl (polyglactin) is a braided synthetic polymeric suture which is absorbable. It handles well and knots are secure because of its braid. It is ideal for bowel anastomoses and tying of ligatures.

Q2
Can you name other examples of polymeric synthetic absorbable sutures?

A2
Yes. Examples include polydioxanone (PDS), polyglycolic acid (Dexon) and polycarbonate (Maoxoan).

Q3
What type of suture is silk? When should it be avoided?

A3
Silk is a natural non-absorbable suture which is braided. It is biodegradable and encourages the formation of suture sinuses and abscesses. Therefore it should be avoided in vascular anastomoses and skin closure.

Q4
What type of suture is recommended for vascular anastomosis and for skin closure?

A4
Polypropylene is used for vascular anastomosis. Skin is usually closed with synthetic non-absorbable sutures of the monofilament type, e.g. polyamide (nylon) and polypropylene (Prolene). Subcuticular Dexon, PDS or Vicryl can also be used for skin closure.

Q5

What type of stapling device is used for creating (a) a side-to-side bowel anastomosis and (b) an end-to-end bowel anastomosis?

A5

1. A linear stapling device (GIA stapler) is used for creating a side-to-side anastomosis. A small enterostomy is created close to the selected anastomosis site to allow the insertion of the separated stapler's jaws. The two handles of the instrument are then locked together and the push bar is actuated. The two handles are then separated and withdrawn, and the enterostomy holes are closed with Vicryl. The stapler inserts four parallel, linear rows of staples and cuts between the two middle rows.

2. A circular stapling device (e.g. an EEA gun) is used for uniting bowel end to end. The bowel ends are drawn over the anvil and the cartridge with a purse string of Prolene. The anvil is approximated to the cartridge and the gun is fired to construct the anastomosis with one or two layers of clips. The gun is opened to separate two ends and twisted to free the anastomosis before withdrawing the stapling device.

Anterior Resection of the Rectum

Q1
Describe the blood and lymphatic supply of the rectum

A1
The upper and middle thirds of the rectum are supplied by the superior rectal artery, a terminal branch of the inferior mesenteric artery. These parts are drained by the superior rectal vein, a tributary of the inferior mesenteric vein (portal circulation). Lymphatic channels parallel the arterial blood supply and drain into the inferior mesenteric nodes.

Q2
What operation would you perform for an operable rectal carcinoma 8 cm away from the anorectal junction?

A2
I would perform an anterior resection of the rectum.

Q3
Describe the main steps of the operation

A3
1. Preoperative preparation:
   - The patient should also consent to a colostomy
   - Sigmoidoscopy and rectal biopsy should be performed
   - A barium enema or colonoscopy is performed in most cases
   - The patient is catheterised
   - DVT (deep vein thrombosis) prophylaxis and broad-spectrum antimicrobials are commenced
2. Anaesthetic is general with endotracheal intubation. This may be supplemented with an epidural anaesthetic
3. Position the patient in the Lloyd-Davies position
4. The whole abdomen is prepared
5. Surgical access is achieved through a long midline incision skirting the umbilicus
6. Procedure:

- The abdomen is assessed in a methodical fashion to define the extent of disease, e.g. hepatic metastases
- The congenital adhesions binding the sigmoid colon to the abdominal wall in the left iliac fossa, and the descending colon to the lateral peritoneum, are divided to mobilise the descending and sigmoid colon. The white line of Todt guides the surgeon to the correct plane of dissection
- The splenic flexure is mobilised (the phrenicocolic ligament is divided). Care is taken not to damage the spleen, the tail of the pancreas and the duodenojejunal junction
- The left ureter and gonadal vessels are identified and preserved. The greater omentum is preserved unless it contains metastases
- The peritoneum over the aorta is incised and the inferior mesenteric artery is identified, clamped, ligated and divided close to its origin. The inferior mesenteric vein is ligated and divided close to the lower border of the pancreas. In atherosclerotic patients the left colic artery is preserved
- The rectum is mobilised by dividing the lateral rectal ligaments and the mesorectum. Damage to the ureter and seminal vesicles within the pelvis should be avoided
- The inferior mesenteric artery is ligated and divided near its origin
- The rectum is then straightened out and drawn out of the pelvis. The level of division should be at least 2 cm away from the tumour, and 5 cm clearance is preferred. Soft and crushing clamps are applied near the level of division; the colon and the rectum are divided between the clamps. The specimen is then removed with its mesentery and lymph nodes, and sent for histological examination
- The cut ends of the rectum and colon are swabbed with a cytocidal solution
- A colorectal anastomosis is constructed using a circular stapling device
- Haemostasis is ensured and peritoneal lavage with sterile water is carried out
- A rectal washout with sterile water is also performed
- The abdominal wall is closed using the mass closure technique with strong looped nylon. The skin is closed with clips or subcutaneous Prolene

Q4
What other incisions can you use for this operation?

A4
A long left paramedian incision.

Q5
When would you prefer to perform a per anal anastomosis?

A5
When the rectum is divided at the level of the puborectalis, as the stapling device removes about 8 mm from the rectal end.

Q6
Assuming that you have constructed your anastomosis, but you are doubtful about the viability of the anastomosis, what would you do?

A6
I would perform a defunctioning transverse loop colostomy or ileostomy

Q7
What are the principles of screening for colorectal cancer?

A7
1. Children with possible familial adenomatous polyposis should have sigmoidoscopy at puberty
2. Annual colonoscopy should begin at the age of 25 for members of families with Lynch syndrome
3. Annual colonoscopy is advisable for patients who have had ulcerative colitis for longer than 10 years
4. Colonoscopy for patients who have a history of colorectal cancer in first-degree relatives
5. Positive faecal occult blood test (using antibody to haemoglobin) is an indication for colonoscopy
6. Surveillance colonoscopy and serum CEA (carcinoembryonic antigen) is usual for patients with a history of colorectal cancer

7. A single colonoscopy or flexible sigmoidoscopy may be performed around the age of 60 years

Q8
What is the treatment of choice for a 3 cm sessile villous adenoma located 13 cm from the anal verge?

A8
This lesion can be excised completely using the transanal endoscopic microsurgery (TEM) technique.

Peritonitis

Q1
Describe briefly the procedure that you would carry out for generalised peritonitis in the absence of localising signs

A1
1. Dehydration is corrected before operation with intravenous fluids
2. Broad-spectrum antibiotics (e.g. cefuroxime and metronidazole) are commenced and a nasogastric tube is passed
3. Preoperative investigations are completed and reviewed, e.g. FBC (full blood count), U+Es (urea and electrolytes), crossmatch, ECG (electrocardiogram), radiographs
4. The anaesthetic is general with endotracheal intubation and epidural anaesthesia
5. The patient is positioned supine
6. The whole abdomen is prepared from nipples to thighs
7. Surgical access is achieved through a long midline incision skirting the umbilicus. Suction is used to remove peritoneal fluid and contaminated material
8. Any free fluid in the peritoneum is noted and a specimen is sent for microbiological examination
9. A quick initial assessment of the abdominal cavity is carried out, followed by a methodical examination of the abdominal contents
10. An attempt is made to identify the cause of the peritonitis, and an appropriate procedure is carried out to deal with the cause
11. The abdominal cavity is washed out with warm saline – up to 15 litres may be used
12. Draining tubes are inserted if necessary, depending on the cause of peritonitis and the procedure performed
13. If there is gross contamination, tubes are left for peritoneal lavage and postoperative drainage
14. *En masse* closure is carried out with strong nylon

Q2
List the causes of generalised peritonitis

A2

1. Acute appendicitis (perforated)
2. Perforated peptic ulcer
3. Perforation of sigmoid diverticulitis
4. Rupture of ectopic pregnancy
5. Acute pancreatitis
6. Perforation of inflamed gallbladder
7. Perforated colon due to carcinoma
8. Primary peritonitis

Q3
What findings at laparotomy suggest acute pancreatitis?

A3

1. Blood-stained peritoneal effusion
2. Whitish plaques of fat necrosis
3. Inflamed pancreas
4. Discoloration of the retroperitoneum

Q4
What organism is commonly responsible for primary peritonitis?

A4
Pneumococcus.

Q5
Which organisms are most commonly responsible for peritonitis due to bowel perforation?

A5
Bacteroides, Escherichia coli, Clostridium perfringens, Pseudomonas and *Klebsiella* are the commonest causative organisms.

Q6
What are the signs and principles of management of dehydration in the preoperative period?

A6

1. Signs of dehydration include:
   - Tachycardia
   - Hypotension
   - Reduced JVP (jugular vein pressure)
   - Reduced skin turgor (inaccurate)
   - Reduced skin temperature
   - Reduced urine output
   - Peripheral shutdown due to vasoconstriction
2. Principles of management
   - Insertion of a central venous catheter to monitor central venous pressure (CVP)
   - Insertion of a nasogastric tube
   - Insertion of a transurethral catheter
   - Intravenous fluid replacement
   - Assessment of FBC and serum U+Es

Q7

What is the normal CVP reading and what reading would you expect in a dehydrated patient?

A7

The normal reading is approximately $+5\,cmH_2O$. In a dehydrated patient the CVP is usually below 0, depending on the severity of dehydration.

Femoral Hernia

Q1
What surgical approach would you use for a strangulated femoral hernia that could not be reduced by conservative methods?

A1
I would use a low approach through a 9 cm incision along the crease of the groin centred midway between the anterior iliac spine and the symphysis pubis.

Q2
What action do you take once you have exposed the hernial sac?

A2
1. The hernial sac is held with two artery forceps and incised. If no bowel is seen in it, this means that the anaesthesia and premedication have succeeded in reducing the hernia. If the hernial sac contains bowel, the bowel is drawn downwards and the ligamentous margins of the sac neck are dilated using the two index fingers, forming a wedge.
2. The bowel is then assessed for viability, with particular attention being paid to the constriction ring. If there is a sheen to its wall, it looks pink, peristalsis is seen and there is mesenteric pulsation, the bowel is returned to the abdomen with the hernial sac contents and a hernial repair is performed. If there is doubt about the bowel viability it is covered with warm moist packs and re-examined 5 minutes later. If the bowel is non-viable the affected segment is resected and anastomosed end to end.
3. Once the sac contents are returned to the abdomen, the sac is transfixed at its neck using Vicryl catgut and excised 1 cm distal to the ligation. The hernia is repaired by uniting the inguinal and pectineal ligaments for 1 cm laterally using a single stitch (figure of eight), or two or three stitches on a J-shaped needle, with a strong monofilamentous nylon suture. Care is taken to protect the laterally located femoral vein and avoid constricting it. The subcutaneous tissue is closed with Vicryl and the skin with subcuticular Prolene.

Q3
If the doubtfully viable bowel slips back into the abdomen and you cannot recover it, what will you do?

A3
I will perform a laparotomy through a lower midline incision.

Q4
What does a small intestinal stenosis of Garré refer to?

A4
It refers to an annular stenotic stricture of the small bowel due to a healing mucosal ulcer caused by a strangulated hernia. This is because the intestinal mucosa is more vulnerable to ischaemia than the overlying seromuscularis, which may survive strangulation. The condition presents with an incipient small bowel obstruction.

Q5
What other surgical approaches to the femoral hernia are there?

A5
1. High approach through an incision 2 cm above the medial two thirds of the inguinal ligament
2. McVedy's approach
3. Henry's approach

Tracheostomy

Q1
Describe briefly the procedure of elective tracheostomy omitting steps like preoperative preparation, anaesthesia, skin preparation and postoperative care

A1
A transverse skin incision is made along a skin crease midway between the cricoid cartilage and the suprasternal notch. The pretracheal muscles are separated, and the thyroid isthmus is divided between clamps and its raw edges are oversewn. Then a 1 cm disc centred on tracheal rings 3 and 4 is cut out. The tracheal tube is inserted and the skin incision is loosely sutured over it.

Q2
In an emergency, would you prefer 'crash' tracheostomy or cricothyroidotomy?

A2
I prefer cricothyroidotomy in almost all cases.

Q3
How would you do it?

A3
The patient is laid back and the neck is extended. A stab incision is made with a scalpel between the cricoid and thyroid cartilages (through the cricothyroid membrane). Once the scalpel has entered the airway, it is removed and a curved (downwards) metal tube is inserted into the trachea. Alternatively, a large-bore needle and cannula can be inserted into the cricothyroid membrane percutaneously.

Q4
Give six postoperative complications of elective tracheostomy?

A4
1. Perichondritis and subglottic stenosis, if the cricoid cartilage is injured

2. Obstruction of the tube or the trachea by secretions
3. Mediastinal emphysema
4. Pneumothorax
5. Dislodgement of the tube, which may be partial or complete
6. Pneumonia

Zadik's Operation

Q1
What operation is suitable for recurrent ingrowing toe nails?

A1
Zadik's operation.

Q2
Name two contraindications for the operation

A2
1. Peripheral vascular disease
2. Sepsis

Q3
How would you perform the operation?

A3
1. Preoperative preparation
   - The site is marked
   - Sepsis and peripheral vascular disease are excluded
   - The patient should be told that the toe nail will never grow back
2. Position of the patient is supine
3. The distal lower leg and foot are cleansed and draped
4. Local ring block anaesthesia with a rubber band (as a digital tourniquet) is used
5. Procedure
   - The nail is removed using a MacDonald's elevator
   - Two incisions (about 1 cm long) are made at each corner of the nail, extending proximally to the level of the interphalangeal joint. The skin and subcutaneous tissue are lifted as a flap. Dissection under the skin incisions (on each side) is carried out to the midlateral line
   - The nail bed is cut transversely at the level of the lunula, and then removed from the proximal phalanx as proximal as the insertion of the extensor tendon so that the whole germinal

matrix is removed
6. Closure
   - It is ascertained that no germinal matrix is left behind
   - The skin flap end is sutured to the nail bed, and skin incisions on either side are closed with nylon
7. Postoperative care
   - A non-adherent dressing is applied
   - A Tubigrip bandage is applied
   - The tourniquet is released
   - The foot is elevated for 24 hours
   - The sutures are removed after 12 days

Colostomy

Q1
Give three indications for performing a transverse colostomy

A1
1. Distal colonic obstruction if the patient is unfit for urgent resection or the cause of the obstruction is inoperable
2. Diverticular disease of the distal colon with abscess formation
3. Colovesical fistula with severe urinary tract infection

Q2
Describe the procedure of a transverse colostomy, excluding steps like preoperative preparation, anaesthesia, etc.

A2
1. A transverse incision (about 9 cm long) is made, centred on the upper right rectus muscle between the costal margin and the umbilicus. The anterior and posterior rectus sheath and the rectus muscle are divided transversely
2. A loop of the proximal transverse colon is drawn into the wound and a hole is made through the mesentery close to the bowel
3. A colostomy rod is passed through the mesentery. A transverse incision is made through the colon for half of its circumference at the apex of the loop
4. The edges of the opened colon are turned back and sutured to the edges of the skin incision with interrupted chromic gut sutures on a cutting needle. Then a colostomy appliance is placed over the loop colostomy rod

Q3
When is the colostomy rod usually removed?

A3
7–10 days after the operation.

Q4
When would you close a temporary colostomy?

A4
A loop colostomy should be closed when it is no longer necessary. It is safer to close the colostomy when the stoma has matured, i.e. 1–2 months after it has been established.

Q5
Do you prefer the intraperitoneal or the extraperitoneal method of closure?

A5
I prefer the intraperitoneal technique as it has fewer complications with faecal fistulae.

Q6
Name seven complications that can occur with a colostomy

A6
1. Stenosis
2. Prolapse
3. Retraction
4. Colostomy diarrhoea, which is usually infective and responds to metronidazole
5. Bleeding from the granulomata around the edge of the colostomy
6. Necrosis of the distal end
7. Paracolostomy hernia

Surgery for Hiatus Hernia

Q1
What open surgical approaches are available for repairing a hiatus hernia?

A1
Two approaches:
1. Transabdominal approach
2. Transthoracic approach (Belsey Mark IV repair)

Q2
Which approach do you prefer?

A2
I prefer the transabdominal approach because it allows a full assessment of intra-abdominal organs. However, in short obese patients, the transthoracic approach may be of benefit.

Q3
What specific surgical procedures can be performed for hiatus hernia?

A3
1. Nissen's fundoplication
2. Anterior gastropexy (Boerema gastropexy)
3. Posterior gastropexy (Hill's procedure)
4. Angelchick prosthesis
5. Belsey Mark IV procedure
6. Collis gastroplasty
7. Oesophageal resection

Q4
Describe the main steps of Nissen's fundoplication

A4

1. An upper midline incision is made
2. A wide-bored orogastric tube is passed
3. A hiatal repair is carried out (anterior or posterior) if possible. The sutures of the repair are not tied until after the fundoplication
4. The lower 6 cm of the oesophagus are separated from the hiatal margins. The gastric fundus is also mobilised by dividing the gastrophrenic ligament and the upper short gastric arteries. The upper part of the lesser curvature is cleared, preserving the nerves of Latarget
5. The freed fundus is then drawn posteriorly around the cardia. Interrupted non-absorbable sutures are passed through the fundus, the oesophageal wall and the anterior gastric wall
6. The hiatal repair sutures are then tied so that the crura fit snugly above the fundoplication
7. The orogastric tube is withdrawn and the wound is closed

Laparoscopic Nissen's Fundoplication

Q1
What are the principles of the laparoscopic Nissen's fundo-plication procedure?

A1
1. The patient is intubated, given general anaesthesia and positioned in the reversed Trendelenburg position
2. Pneumoperitoneum is established and five ports are inserted: one in the supraumbilical position (10 mm), one in the right subcostal area, one in the left subcostal area, one at the midpoint between the first and third ports, and one near the xiphisternum
3. Dissection of the oesophageal hiatus is performed following division of the lesser omentum and retraction of the right lobe of the liver
4. The gastric wrap (approximately 5 cm long) is passed behind the oesophagus
5. The greater curvature is devascularised by dividing the short gastric arteries between clips or using diathermy
6. A 33 Fr Malony dilator is introduced through the gastro-oesophageal junction
7. The gastric wrap is sutured with interrupted silk sutures (approximately five), which also pass through the oesophageal wall

Q2
What are the main advantages of this procedure over open Nissen's fundoplication?

A2
1. Reduced hospital stay. The median length of hospital stay in most cases is 3 days (cf. 10 days for the open procedure)
2. Lower incidence of postoperative morbidity
3. It has the same success rate as the open procedure

Q3
What tests can be carried out to assess the success of Nissen's fundoplication?

A3
1. Upper gastrointestinal endoscopy
2. Oesophageal pH manometry

Q4
Outline the principles of medical treatment of gastro-oesophageal reflux

A4
1. Life-style changes include raising the head of the bed, weight reduction, avoidance of alcohol, cessation of smoking and avoidance of aggravating foods
2. Antacids and alginates
3. H_2-antagonists and motility stimulants
4. Proton pump inhibitors such as lansoprazole (15–30 mg daily) for stricturing and erosive cases

Circumcision

Q1
What are the medical indications for circumcision?

A1
1. Phimosis
2. Recurrent balanitis
3. Squamous cell carcinoma of the foreskin
4. Paraphimosis

Q2
What are the causes of phimosis?

A2
1. Congenital phimosis is due to congenital adhesions between the foreskin and the glans. It is not normally possible to retract the foreskin in the first year of life
2. Acquired phimosis is commonly due to balanitis xerotica obliterans. Phimosis can also be senile

Q3
Describe the procedure (only) of a circumcision

A3
1. The foreskin is gently freed from the glans so that it can be retracted fully (a silver probe or an artery forceps is used). Non-irritant solutions are used for cleansing
2. The foreskin is pulled down and two straight artery forceps are applied side by side on the dorsal surface of the foreskin in the midline. The foreskin is then divided between these two forceps up to about 4 mm away from the corona
3. From the apex of this incision, the foreskin is incised laterally and circumferentially towards the frenum (on both sides)
4. The frenum is held with an artery forceps and the foreskin is excised. The frenum is then transfixed using catgut suture
5. Haemostasis is ensured using fine catgut and bipolar diathermy.

Unipolar diathermy is never used
6. The two layers of skin are brought together with a few sutures
7. Use of dressings is avoided; when used they are applied very loosely

Q4
Is there a different circumcision technique for infants?

A4
Yes, using the Plastibell (Hollister) instrument. The foreskin is freed and retracted. The Plastibell is slipped over the glans penis and the foreskin is ligated and divided in the groove of the instrument, then the foreskin is cut and removed.

Q5
What are the complications of circumcision?

A5
1. Bleeding and haematoma formation
2. Infection
3. Acute urinary retention
4. Psychological morbidity
5. Urethrocutaneous fistula
6. Meatal stenosis
7. Ischaemia and necrosis of the distal part of the penis

Orchidectomy

Q1
Describe the orchidectomy procedure you would carry out for testicular cancer, excluding preoperative preparation and postoperative care

A1
1. The position of the patient is supine
2. Skin preparation includes the inguinal region, scrotum, penis and the upper thighs. Drapes should expose the inguinal region on the affected side and allow easy access to the scrotum
3. An incision is made 2 cm above (and parallel to) the medial two thirds of the inguinal ligaments starting medially at the pubic tubercle
4. The external oblique muscle is identified and split along its fibres (over the length of the wound). The spermatic cord is identified and freed from the inguinal canal by blunt dissection, then it is cross-clamped with two artery forceps at the internal ring and divided between the clamps. The cord is tied with strong chromic catgut
5. The testicle is gently manipulated into the inguinal region and freed from the scrotum by blunt dissection
6. The external oblique aponeurosis is closed with absorbable sutures. The skin is closed with subcuticular Prolene and scrotal support is applied

Q2
Why is the inguinal approach preferred to the scrotal one in orchidectomy for testicular cancer?

A2
The inguinal approach (with early clamping and division of the spermatic cord) is associated with a lower incidence of recurrence in the scrotum and regional lymph nodes.

Q3
What staging system do you use for testicular tumours?

A3
I use the Royal Marsden Hospital staging system:

Stage I: Tumour confined to the testis, no distant metastases
Stage II: Involvement of the infradiaphragmatic lymph nodes (substages A, B and C)
Stage III: Infradiaphragmatic and supradiaphragmatic lymph nodes are involved (substages A, B and C)
Stage IV: Extralymphatic tissue is involved (H for hepatic metastases and L for lung metastases)

Q4
What is the treatment of choice for a patient with stage III seminoma?

A4
Combination chemotherapy (bleomycin, etoposide and cisplatin) and/or radiotherapy.

Q5
What types of orchidectomy are there?

A5
1. Radical orchidectomy through an inguinal incision (as described earlier)
2. Simple orchidectomy through a transverse scrotal incision
3. Subcapsular orchidectomy

Q6
Give an indication for bilateral simple orchidectomy

A6
Advanced prostatic carcinoma.

Q7
Can you think of a disadvantage for subcapsular orchidectomy performed as part of the treatment for advanced prostatic carcinoma?

A7
Yes. The remaining epididymis may secrete androgen.

Inguinal Herniorrhaphy

Q1
Describe the procedure of inguinal herniorrhaphy in an adult (male)

A1
1. The patient is positioned supine
2. The anaesthetic is general or local
3. An incision is made approximately 2.5 cm above the medial two thirds of the inguinal ligament, preferably along a skin crease (Langer's lines). The superficial veins are ligated and divided
4. The external oblique is slit along its fibres (using scissors) as far as the superficial inguinal ring. The spermatic cord is identified and the external spermatic fascia is incised. The spermatic muscle fibres may be divided. A tape is passed around the cord
5. The spermatic cord is inspected for the presence of an indirect hernial sac; if found, the sac is held with clips and separated from the spermatic cord structures as far as the deep inguinal ring
6. The sac is opened and its contents are released into the abdominal cavity. The sac is then transfixed close to the deep ring (chromic catgut or Vicryl is used) and divided just distal to the ligature
7. The posterior wall of the inguinal canal is reinforced using Prolene mesh. The mesh is applied on the transversalis fascia and internal oblique muscle. The lateral end is slit in the middle to accommodate the spermatic cord. The inferior margin of the mesh is sutured onto the inner surface of the inguinal ligament using continuous Prolene or nylon suture. The medial and superior margins are fixed to the rectus sheath and internal oblique muscle using interrupted sutures. The medial end should reach the pubic tubercle. The tail ends (lateral) are sutured to one another around the cord
8. The external oblique aponeurosis is then closed with a continuous absorbable suture (e.g. Vicryl). The Scarpa's fascia and the skin are closed and the ipsilateral testicle is drawn downwards

Q2
What other types of repair have you used?

A2
1. Shouldice repair
2. Laparoscopic preperitoneal mesh repair
3. Darn repair

Q3
What is the incidence of recurrence for Shouldice repair?

A3
The recurrence rate is < 1% at the Shouldice Clinic, but it approaches 3.5% elsewhere.

Q4
How can you explain this difference?

A4
At the Shouldice Clinic, the trainee surgeon is required to assist in at least 50 herniorrhaphies and then perform 100 herniorrhaphies (at least) under supervision before being allowed to repair inguinal hernias independently. These training criteria are not met elsewhere.

Q5
What are the main advantages and disadvantages of prosthetic mesh repair?

A5
Advantages:

1. The procedure is easier to learn and perform
2. It has a lower recurrence rate (< 1%)
3. There is a lower analgesic requirement

The main disadvantage is the risk of infection. The incidence can be reduced by avoiding haematomas and using prophylactic antibiotics.

Q6
What are the main indications for laparoscopic inguinal hernia repair?

A6

Laparoscopic repair is indicated in bilateral inguinal hernias and in recurrent hernias.

Varicose Vein Surgery

Q1
What incision would you make to gain access to the saphenofemoral junction during Trendelenburg's operation?

A1
Access is provided through a short oblique incision parallel to and below the inguinal ligament, 2 cm below and 2 cm lateral to the pubic tubercle along the groin crease.

Q2
What tributaries of the long saphenous vein would you encounter during the operation?

A2
1. Superficial inferior epigastric vein
2. Deep external pudendal vein
3. Superficial external pudendal vein
4. Superficial circumflex iliac vein
5. Anterolateral and posteromedial thigh veins

Q3
How is the stripping of the long saphenous vein carried out?

A3
The long saphenous vein (near the saphenofemoral junction) and its tributaries are ligated and divided. A ligature is placed around the long saphenous trunk and held so that the lumen of the vein is occluded. In the meantime a side hole is made in the vein proximal to the tie. Then the tip of the stripper (of appropriate size) is passed down the vein through the hole, and advanced to about 5 cm below the knee. An oblique incision about 1.5 cm long is made over the tip of the stripper. The vein at this point is dissected out from surrounding structures and tied off distally. Then the vein is incised to deliver the tip of the stripper. The stripper is then pulled down (using a T-shaped handle) so that the vein is stripped from the groin to below the knee. Bleeding is minimised by applying a crepe bandage and pressure as the stripper is withdrawn.

Q4
How do you perform multiple phlebectomies (avulsions) of varicose veins?

A4
1. Accurate marking of varicosities is essential before the operation
2. Small stab incisions (vertical) are made over the varicosities
3. A loop of vein is drawn out through the stab incision by blunt dissection using artery forceps (mosquitoes) or a special hook
4. The loop of vein is held between two artery forceps and divided. Using traction and rotation the vein is pulled until it breaks. Bleeding is controlled by local pressure
5. Skin incisions are closed with Steri-Strips, other adhesive means or sutures

Q5
What are the main complications of varicose veins?

A5
1. Eczematous skin changes and ulceration
2. Haemorrhage
3. Superficial thrombophlebitis
4. Pain
5. Periostitis
6. Calcification
7. Psychological complications

Intussusception/Meconium Ileus

Q1
What are the main abdominal causes of acute surgical admission in infants?

A1
1. Strangulated inguinal hernia
2. Hypertrophic pyloric stenosis
3. Intussusception
4. Swallowed foreign body

Q2
Describe the operative procedure you would perform for an intussusception that has failed to respond to conservative reduction using barium enema

A2
1. The patient must be adequately resuscitated before the operation. Broad-spectrum antibiotics are commenced and measures are taken to avoid hypothermia. The bowel is decompressed via a nasogastric tube
2. General anaesthesia is used with endotracheal intubation
3. The patient is positioned supine
4. The abdomen is prepared and draped appropriately
5. A transverse supraumbilical incision is made (about 1 cm above the umbilicus) extending from the midline laterally across the right rectus and oblique muscles. The subcutaneous fat and muscle are cut with diathermy
6. The abdominal cavity is assessed and the intussusception is identified, usually as a sausage-shaped mass in the midline
7. The intussuscipiens is squeezed out in a direction opposite to that of peristalsis so that the intussusceptum is pushed out. The bowel is then assessed and, if non-viable, the ischaemic part is resected and anastomosed end to end
8. Abnormalities acting as lead points for the intussusception are searched for (e.g. Meckel's diverticulum, polyps, cysts)
9. The fascia and muscles are repaired *en masse* with continuous Vicryl,

34

and the skin is closed with a subcuticular absorbable suture

Q3
What operation would you perform for an infant with an inguinal hernia?

A3
I would perform an inguinal herniotomy through the inguinal canal.

Q4
What are the main causes of abdominal emergencies occurring in the newborn?

A4
1. Malrotation of the gut
2. Atresias and stenoses of the gut
3. Anorectal atresia
4. Meconium plugging
5. Meconium ileus
6. Hirschsprung's disease
7. Diaphragmatic hernia
8. Gastroschisis and exomphalos
9. Necrotising enterocolitis

Q5
Very briefly, describe the operative procedure you would perform for meconium ileus

A5
1. A transverse supraumbilical incision is made about 1 cm above the umbilicus. The subcutaneous fat and muscles are cut using diathermy. The umbilical vein is identified, ligated and divided. Then the peritoneum is incised
2. The abdominal cavity is assessed, then the area of obstruction is identified and resected. The distended bowel is decompressed by irrigation with warm normal saline. A Bishop–Koop chimney anastomosis is made. The muscles and fascia are closed *en masse* using

a continuous Vicryl suture. The skin is closed with subcuticular absorbable sutures

Parotid Gland Surgery

Q1
Describe briefly the main steps in the superficial parotidectomy procedure

A1
1. The patient is given a general anaesthetic and positioned supine with a slight head-up tilt
2. An S-shaped cervicomastoidofacial incision is made. The upper part of the incision is made along the pre-auricular groove from the upper part of the zygomatic arch to the lower limit of the ear lobe. This incision is deepened down to the bony external auditory meatus. The incision is curved around the ear lobe to extend for 2–3 cm into the postauricular groove, then angled acutely over the mastoid to be continuous with the cervical part of the incision which is made along an appropriate skin crease in the neck. The cervical incision is extended down to the external jugular vein and deepened through the subcutaneous fat and platysma muscle down to the stylohyoid muscle. The anterior branch of the great auricular nerve is usually sacrificed and a resected segment of it is preserved
3. The trunk and main divisions of the facial nerve are identified
4. The divisions and branches of the facial nerve (temporal, zygomatic, buccal, mandibular and cervical branches) are carefully dissected off by reflecting forwards the overlying parotid tissue as far as the superior and anterior borders of the gland
5. The skin flaps are raised superiorly to just above the zygomatic arch, anteriorly to the anterior border of the masseter muscle and inferiorly to the anterior border of the sternomastoid muscle
6. The parotid duct is dissected forwards as far as the anterior border of the masseter muscle. At this point, it is ligated and divided
7. The superficial parotid is removed having ensured that the five branches of the facial nerve are left undamaged
8. Haemostasis is achieved and a suction drain (e.g. Exudrain) is left in the wound bed. Skin is closed with interrupted nylon sutures

Q2

Give two indications for superficial parotidectomy

A2
1. Benign tumours confined to the superficial part of the parotid gland
2. Recurrent parotitis due to calculi inaccessible through the oral approach

Q3
What operation would you perform for a lump in the deep part of the parotid gland?

A3
I would perform a total parotidectomy preserving all the branches of the facial nerve.

Q4
Describe briefly the parotid duct stomatoplasty procedure

A4
1. The operation is usually performed under general anaesthetic in the supine position. A pernasal tube and pharyngeal packs are used
2. The patient's mouth is kept open with a dental prop, and the tongue is retracted to the contralateral side by an assistant
3. The parotid papilla is identified in the inner side of the cheek opposite the upper second molar tooth
4. Two stay sutures are placed, one above the papilla and one below it. These sutures are pulled with clips by an assistant
5. A lacrimal duct dilator is passed through the parotid duct and a horizontal incision is made extending from the duct orifice posteriorly for about 1.5 cm down to the dilator, which is then removed
6. The two mucosal layers created by the incision (buccal and ductal) are united with interrupted absorbable sutures

Adrenalectomy

Q1
Describe briefly the procedure of right adrenalectomy

A1
1. The procedure is usually performed under general anaesthetic with endotracheal intubation
2. The patient is positioned supine
3. The abdomen is prepared and draped appropriately
4. A transverse supraumbilical incision is made with an upwards convexity
5. A complete laparotomy with a thorough examination of the abdominal contents is carried out
6. The right colic flexure is mobilised and retracted downwards. The liver is retracted upwards
7. The posterior part of the peritoneum is incised just above the level of the upper pole of the right kidney. Then the right adrenal gland is identified. It is separated from the kidney with the perinephric fat and fascia
8. The gland is gently dissected off the inferior vena cava (IVC) and its vein is ligated and divided near its entry into the IVC. The adrenal arteries are diathermised with electrical cautery and divided
9. The lateral aspect of the gland is bluntly dissected out and the gland is removed
10. Haemostasis is ensured and the wound is closed in layers

Q2
You have described an anterior transperitoneal approach. What other approaches are possible?

A2
1. The lateral approach through the bed of the 12th rib
2. The thoracoabdominal approach through the bed of the 10th (left) or the 11th (right) rib
3. The posterior approach through the bed of the 11th or 12th rib on each side

4.   The laparoscopic approach

Q3
What specific preoperative preparation is required when the operation is carried out for phaeochromocytoma?

A3
1.   Blockade of α-adrenergic receptors with phenoxybenzamine or phentolamine
2.   Blockade of β-receptors with atenolol if there is cardiac dysrhythmia or marked tachycardia
3.   Restoration of circulating blood volume

Q4
What postoperative maintenance therapy is commonly prescribed for bilateral adrenalectomy patients?

A4
1.   Oral hydrocortisone 30 mg per day (100 mg given intravenously three times a day in the immediate postoperative period)
2.   Fludrocortisone 0.1 mg daily

Embolectomy and Arterial Grafts

Q1
What vascular procedure is a Fogarty catheter used for?

A1
It is used for embolectomy or thrombectomy.

Q2
What are the principles of an embolectomy?

A2
1. The patient is fully heparinised
2. Anaesthetic may be general or local
3. A suitable size of Fogarty catheter is selected
4. The involved artery is exposed and an arteriotomy is made
5. The uninflated catheter is passed beyond the site of the clot, then the balloon is inflated and the catheter is pulled through the arteriotomy, where the embolus is recovered. This manoeuvre is repeated until free flow of blood is achieved
6. The same procedure is carried out in the other direction
7. Heparinised saline is introduced into the vessels through the arteriotomy, which is then closed with Prolene sutures. A small suction drain is left at the site of arteriotomy and the wound is closed

Q3
If there is a propagated thrombus causing the ischaemia, what adjunctive procedure would you use in addition to Fogarty thrombectomy?

A3
I would infuse a thrombolytic agent such as streptokinase, tPA (tissue plasminogen activator) or urokinase intra-arterially in order to restore patency.

Q4
What is the graft of choice for a femoropopliteal bypass and a

femorodistal bypass?

A4

1. Reversed autogenous long saphenous vein graft for femoro-popliteal bypass
2. *In situ* long saphenous vein graft for femorodistal bypass

Q5

Name a synthetic graft used for femoropopliteal bypass procedures. What are the complications of such grafts?

A5

Expanded polytetrafluoroethylene (PTFE). The complications include:

1. Haemorrhage
2. Infection
3. Suture-line aneurysm
4. Graft failure due to thrombosis or pseudointimal fibrous hyperplasia

Laparoscopic Cholecystectomy

Q1
How do you perform a laparoscopic cholecystectomy?

A1
1. Preoperative procedure
   - The patient's consent is obtained to both laparoscopic and open cholecystectomy
   - Investigations are reviewed, e.g. FBC (full blood count), U+Es (urea and electrolytes), LFTs (liver function tests), ultrasonography of the biliary tree and ERCP (endoscopic retrograde cholangiopancreatography) if performed
   - Prophylactic antimicrobials are started prior to surgery, e.g. cefuroxime and metronidazole
   - Appropriate DVT (deep vein thrombosis) prophylaxis is started, e.g. subcutaneous heparin 5000 i.u. twice a day
   - All laparoscopic equipment is checked
2. Anaesthetic is general with endotracheal intubation. A nasogastric tube is passed
3. The patient is placed in the Trendelenburg position
4. The abdomen is prepared and draped appropriately
5. Procedure
   - A Veress needle is passed subumbilically, and a pneumo-peritoneum is created using an insufflator set to deliver 1 litre of carbon dioxide per minute initially, then about 5 litre/min
   - The Veress needle is then removed and a 10 mm trocar and cannula are passed through the subumbilical incision. A 10 mm 0° diagnostic laparoscope attached to a video camera is passed through the cannula
   - Alternatively, the pneumoperitoneum is created through the 10 mm subumbilical port, which is made in the intraperitoneal cavity using an open approach under direct vision
   - The patient is then changed to the reverse Trendelenburg position with left rotation
   - Three ports are created under direct vision, one (10 mm) in the epigastrium (midline) and two of 5 mm in the right quadrant (midclavicular and anterior axillary positions)

- The cystic duct and artery are bluntly dissected through the epigastric port
- The lateral and midclavicular ports are used to grasp the gallbladder, which is retracted cephalad and towards the abdominal wall
- Once the cystic artery and ducts are clearly dissected, they are double clipped using a multiple clip applicator and divided between the clips
- The gallbladder is dissected from the hepatic bed using an NdYAG laser or diathermy hook to maintain haemostasis. It is removed through the epigastric or subumbilical incision, and the operating field is irrigated and aspirated using saline
- A suction drain is left in the subhepatic bed and passed through the lateral portal if indicated
- The pneumoperitoneum is released
- Abdominal incisions are closed using Vicryl for subcutaneous closure and Steri-Strips or nylon for skin

Q2
When would you perform an intraoperative cholangiogram during laparoscopic cholecystectomy?

A2
The indications for intraoperative cholangiography include:

1. History of jaundice for more than 2 days
2. Diameter of the common bile duct (CBD) greater than 7 mm on preoperative ultrasonography
3. Abnormal liver function tests

However, as I am not skilled in performing intraoperative cholangiography during laparoscopic cholecystectomy, I prefer arranging a preoperative cholangiogram, e.g. ERCP after ultrasound investigation

Q3
Is it essential to pass a nasogastric tube and a urinary catheter?

A3
No. Some laparoscopic surgeons do not use either.

Q4
What is the usual postoperative course?

A4
1. The nasogastric tube is removed in the recovery room
2. Analgesia is prescribed as requested, e.g. diclofenac or opiates
3. The drain is removed when drainage is minimal
4. The patient is usually discharged the next day
5. The patient returns to normal activity in 6 days and to work in 10 days
6. Skin sutures are removed in 7–10 days

Q5
What complications may arise?

A5
1. Perforation of the gallbladder
2. Haemorrhage
3. Slipping of clips on the cystic duct and artery
4. Damage to the duodenum
5. Wound hernia and intestinal obstruction
6. Bile duct injury
7. Leakage from the accessory hepatic duct
8. Sepsis
9. Diathermy injuries to distant organs
10. Pneumomediastinum or pneumothorax
11. Deep vein thrombosis and pulmonary embolism

Q6
Give four contraindications

A6
1. Severe adhesions owing to previous surgery
2. Pregnancy

3. Severe chronic obstructive airway disease
4. Suspected carcinoma of the gallbladder

Q7
Can you think of two disadvantages of laparoscopic chole-cystectomy?

A7
1. Higher incidence of CBD injury
2. The learning curve is slow rising

Breast Cancer Surgery

Q1
What surgical procedure would you perform on a 57-year-old woman with a 3 cm carcinoma in the upper outer quadrant of the left breast? (The ipsilateral axillary nodes are impalpable)

A1
I would perform a wide local excision combined with a level III axillary dissection.

Q2
Describe the procedure of wide local excision

A2
1. The lump is marked and informed consent is obtained
2. Lumpectomy can be performed under general or local anaesthetic. The former is used if axillary dissection is also required
3. A circumferential incision is made over the lump
4. Skin flaps are elevated for a few centimetres
5. The lump is excised with an approximate 1.5 cm margin of healthy tissue. The deep margin of the excision should reach the pectoral fascia
6. Meticulous haemostasis is ensured and the skin is closed with a subcuticular suture

Q3
What is meant by quadrantectomy and what are the advantages and disadvantages of the procedure?

A3
In quadrantectomy, an ellipse of the overlying skin and the underlying pectoral fascia are removed, in addition to the wide local excision of the lump. Quadrantectomy has a lower recurrence rate than lumpectomy, but the cosmesis is inferior to that of lumpectomy.

Q4
What are the anatomical limits of the various levels of axillary dissection?

A4
Level 1 dissection removes axillary nodes lateral to the pectoralis minor muscle. Level II nodes lie behind the pectoralis minor muscle. Level III nodes lie medial to the medial border of the muscle.

Q5
What are the aims of axillary dissection?

A5
1. To reduce the axillary recurrence rate
2. To establish a prognosis (staging)
3. To decide whether chemotherapy is necessary

Q6
What are the possible complications of axillary dissection?

A6
1. Haematoma
2. Wound infection
3. Seroma formation (common)
4. Frozen-shoulder syndrome
5. Intercostobrachial neuralgia
6. Lymphoedema (incidence 7%)
7. Injury to the thoracodorsal nerve, long thoracic nerve, axillary vein or brachial plexus

Mastectomy

Q1
How do you perform a simple mastectomy? (Describe the procedure only, excluding other steps)

A1
1. A transverse elliptical incision is made encompassing about 5 cm of skin around the lesion and also the nipple. The skin and subcutaneous fat are elevated as flaps. Care is taken not to traumatise the skin edges and not to make the skin too thin with buttonholing
2. The upper flap is raised to the upper limit of the breast, and the lower flap is raised to the lower limits of the breast using a pair of dissected scissors or a scalpel
3. Dissection at the upper end of the breast is carried out until the fascia of the pectoralis major is seen and a plane of cleavage is found between the breast and pectoralis major. The dissection is continued downwards to the lower limit of the breast. The main blood vessels entering or leaving the fascia are controlled during this dissection with coagulation diathermy or ligatures. The breast tissue is then elevated from medial to lateral and removed. The specimen is sent for histological examination

Q2
What are the anatomical limits of breast excision?

A2
2 cm below the clavicle superiorly, the sternum medially, the latissimus dorsi muscle laterally, and the upper part of the rectus muscle inferiorly.

Q3
When raising the skin flaps, what is your plane of dissection?

A3
The plane of dissection should correspond to Scarpa's fascia between the subcutaneous fat and mammary fat.

Q4
What does Patey's mastectomy entail?

A4
Simple mastectomy combined with axillary clearance.

Q5
Is your incision always transverse?

A5
No. Depending on the site of the tumour, the incision can be modified; it may be oblique.

Q6
Describe your method of closure

A6
1. Haemostasis is ensured
2. Two vacuum drains (e.g. Exudrains) are placed – one at the axillary end, and the other at the medial end, of the wound. The drains pierce the skin about 2 cm below the incision
3. Skin is closed using 3/0 Prolene on a straight needle if there is no excessive tension. Otherwise, a few subcutaneous absorbable sutures are used, the first of which is placed at the middle of the wound. If skin apposition is not possible, a split-thickness skin graft should be considered
4. Once the skin is closed, the vacuum system is activated and direct pressure is used to evacuate any blood or air until the skin sticks to the underlying tissue. This manoeuvre prevents the formation of postoperative haematoma

Q7
What are the current indications for mastectomy as a treatment for breast carcinoma?

A7
1. Multifocal ductal carcinoma *in situ* (DCIS)

2. Extensive DCIS (> 35 mm)
3. Large (> 5 cm) or centrally located carcinoma (the size of the breast should be taken into account)
4. Patient's request
5. Recurrent carcinoma
6. Paget's disease of the breast
7. Unusual malignancies, e.g. squamous cell carcinoma, sarcoma

Q8
Describe the main steps in the axillary dissection procedure

A8
1. A transverse axillary incision is made
2. The lateral border of the pectoralis major muscle is identified and retracted upwards
3. The shoulder is flexed and abducted, and the elbow is flexed so that the forearm lies across the patient's face
4. The inferior border of the axillary vein is exposed using a blunt dissection, and is selected as the upper limit of the dissection
5. The axillary contents are stroked away from the subscapularis muscle and chest wall using a blunt instrument covered with a gauze swab
6. The thoracodorsal nerve to the latissimus dorsi is identified and preserved
7. The long thoracic nerve is also identified and preserved in the posteromedial aspect of the dissection close to the chest wall
8. The intercostobrachial nerve may be divided as it crosses the midaxillary region
9. The axillary contents are removed and the apical node is marked with a silk suture
10. Bleeding is controlled and a suction drain (e.g. Exudrain) is placed in the axillary bed
11. The skin is closed with subcuticular Prolene on a straight needle
12. After the application of a dressing, the Exudrain is activated
13. For a level III dissection, the pectoralis minor insertion into the coracoid process is divided to retrieve level III nodes

Q9
When is the axillary drain removed?

A9

The drain is usually removed when the 24 hour output is less than 40 ml. However, if the output remains high 7 days after the operation, the drain can still be removed and any axillary seroma that ensues aspirated using a needle and syringe.

Q10

What does the long thoracic nerve innervate?

A10

The serratus anterior muscle. Paralysis of this muscle results in winging of the scapula.

Hartmann's Operation

Q1
Give three indications for Hartmann's procedure

A1
1. Obstructing rectosigmoid carcinoma
2. First stage surgery for sigmoid volvulus
3. Perforated sigmoid colon

Q2
How do you perform the procedure?

A2
1. Preoperative preparation
   - Dehydration and electrolyte disturbances are corrected
   - The patient should give consent for colostomy as well
   - Prophylactic antibacterials are commenced, e.g. intravenous cefuroxime and metronidazole
   - A nasogastric tube is passed
   - The patient is catheterised to empty the bladder and monitor urine output
   - Subcutaneous heparin 5000 units twice daily is commenced
   - The bowel is not usually prepared as the operation is performed as an emergency
2. The anaesthetic is general with endotracheal intubation. This may be supplemented with an epidural anaesthetic
3. The position of the patient is supine with a slight Trendelenburg tilt
4. The whole abdomen is prepared and draped appropriately
5. Surgical access is gained through a long midline incision skirting the umbilicus
6. The abdominal cavity is examined methodically to assess the nature and extent of disease:
   - If there is gross contamination a sample is sent to the microbiology laboratory and peritoneal lavage is performed using warm normal saline, betadine or antiseptic solution
   - The sigmoid colon is mobilised
   - The inferior mesenteric artery branches to the sigmoid colon are

ligated and divided
- The upper third of the rectum is mobilised and care is taken not to injure the left ureter
- Two soft bowel clamps are applied to the distal descending colon and upper third of the rectum
- Two crushing bowel clamps are applied within 2 cm between the two soft clamps. The colon and rectum are divided between the soft and crushing clamps and the specimen is removed and sent for histological examination
- The rectal stump is closed in two layers
- The descending colon end with the soft clamp still applied is brought out through a circular 3 cm incision midway between the anterior superior iliac spine and the umbilicus
- If there has been gross contamination, a corrugated drain is left in the pelvis after the peritoneal lavage
- The wound (except the skin) is closed *en masse* with strong looped nylon
- The skin is closed with Prolene (3/0) on a straight needle
- An end colostomy is fashioned using interrupted circumferential absorbable sutures
7. Postoperative management
- The nasogastric tube is removed when aspirate is minimal
- FBC (full blood count) and U+Es (urea and electrolytes) are determined
- The patient is started on sips of water when bowel sounds return and solids when faeces are passed per colostomy
- Microbiology and histology results are reviewed

Q3
What are the main complications of this operation?

A3
1. Pelvic abscess
2. Wound infection
3. Septicaemia
4. Colostomy complications such as retraction, stenosis, necrosis, prolapse and paracolostomy hernia
5. Damage to the ureter or gonadal vessels
6. 'Blow out' of the distal stump and fistula formation

7. Bowel obstruction due to adhesions or strangulation through the lateral space if this is not closed

8. General complications of surgery such as respiratory complications, DVT (deep vein thrombosis), UTI (urinary tract infection)

Q4
When should Hartmann's procedure be reversed?

A4
The procedure should be reversed when the patient has recovered completely. The incidence of complications (such as anastomotic leak) may be reduced by performing the reversal six months after Hartmann's operation.

Perforated Peptic Ulcer

Q1
How would you repair a perforated peptic ulcer?

A1
1. Preoperative preparation
   - Dehydration is corrected
   - Pain is controlled
   - Investigations are reviewed:
     - Plain radiographs, which are abnormal in about 75% of cases
     - Amylase levels (300–1000 U/litre)
     - Full blood count
   - Antibiotics are commenced
   - A nasogastric tube is passed
2. Anaesthetic is general with endotracheal intubation
3. The position of the patient is supine
4. Skin preparation: all the abdomen is prepared and draped as for an upper abdominal operation
5. An upper midline incision is made from the xiphisternum to the umbilicus
6. Procedure
   - Wound edges are retracted by an assistant
   - Any free fluid is aspirated and a sample is sent for microbiological studies
   - The stomach (especially the lesser curvature) and the duodenum are assessed carefully
   - The perforated ulcer is identified and a biopsy from its edge is taken and sent for histology
   - A two-layered closure of the ulcer is carried out using absorbable sutures, e.g. Vicryl
   - Any free fluid is aspirated from above and below the liver, the lesser sac, the paracolic gutters and the pelvis, and a peritoneal washout with warm normal saline is carried out
   - Definitive treatment for the ulcer in the form of truncal vagotomy and drainage or partial gastrectomy may be carried out if indicated

Q2

How would you manage the patient after the operation?

A2
1. The nasogastric tube is removed when the aspirate is minimal
2. Oral fluids are commenced when the patient passes flatus per rectum
3. H_2-antagonists or omeprazole are commenced
4. The histology report is reviewed

Q3
Name four conditions that may have a similar clinical presentation

A3
1. Acute pancreatitis
2. Acute cholecystitis
3. Leaking aortic aneurysm
4. Myocardial infarction

Q4
Name four features of pneumoperitoneum on plain radiographs

A4
1. Visualisation of the falciform ligament of the liver
2. Visualisation of the lateral wall of the large bowel
3. Visualisation of free air under the hemidiaphragms (erect chest films)
4. Visualisation of the liver

Q5
If you cannot find a perforated peptic ulcer at laparotomy, what would you do?

A5
I would explore all abdominal organs including the gallbladder and sigmoid colon. Other causes of acute abdomen should be excluded during exploration.

Q6
Does the absence of subdiaphragmatic air on an erect chest radiograph exclude a perforated peptic ulcer?

A6
No. There is no radiological evidence of free gas under the hemi-diaphragms in approximately 20% of cases.

Q7
If perforation is found to be associated with bleeding at laparotomy, what would you do?

A7
If there is a bleeding perforated gastric ulcer, I would perform distal gastrectomy. In a perforated anterior duodenal ulcer, the bleeding may be from a coexisting posterior duodenal ulcer. If so, I would insert non-absorbable sutures at the base of the bleeding ulcer and close the anterior gastroduodenotomy as a pyloroplasty. A truncal vagotomy may also be performed.

Pyloric Stenosis

Q1
Describe Ramstedt's pyloromyotomy

A1
1. Preoperative preparation
   - Correction of dehydration and electrolyte disturbance
   - Aspiration of the stomach via a nasogastric tube
2. A general anaesthetic is usually used with endotracheal intubation. Local anaesthetic may be used
3. The position of the patient is supine with protection from cold
4. Procedure
   - A transverse incision (3–4 cm long) is made high in the right hypochondrium midway between the inferior margin of the liver and the costal margin. The incision ends about 1.5 cm from the midline
   - The subcutaneous tissue and muscle are divided by a cutting diathermy
   - The peritoneum is opened and the liver is retracted upwards
   - The greater curvature of the body of the stomach is delivered into the wound and the pyloric 'tumour' is identified
   - An incision is made in the anterior surface of the tumour through the pyloric canal starting distally from the vein of Mayo
   - The hypertrophied muscle fibres are split along the incision down to the mucosa by a blunt artery forceps
   - Air is introduced into the stomach through the nasogastric tube and any leak at the site of incision signifies a mucosal perforation
5. The muscle and fascia are closed *en masse* using interrupted absorbable sutures and the skin is closed using a subcuticular absorbable suture
6. Postoperative care
   - Intravenous fluids for about 18 hours
   - Oral feeds are introduced at 12 hours

Q2
What would you do if the mucosa perforated during pyloromyotomy?

A2

I would repair the perforation with interrupted absorbable sutures.

Q3

What metabolic disturbances are most likely to occur before operation?

A3

1. Hypokalaemia
2. Hypochloraemia
3. Metabolic alkalosis (reduced plasma bicarbonate concentration)
4. Dehydration
5. Raised plasma urea and haematocrit
6. Hyponatraemia
7. Concentrated urine initially alkaline and later acid

Q4

Name four conditions that may have a similar presentation to congenital pyloric stenosis

A4

1. Gastroenteritis
2. Duodenal atresia
3. Volvulus neonatorum
4. Cranial injury at birth

Open Cholecystectomy

Q1
How would you perform an open cholecystectomy?

A1
1. Preoperative preparation
   - All investigations are checked: ultrasound, liver function tests, hepatitis serology (if the patient recently had jaundice), oral cholecystogram, preoperative cholangiogram (if available), plasma urea and electrolytes and clotting (if there is jaundice)
   - Informed consent
   - If the patient is jaundiced, vitamin K, prophylactic broad-spectrum antibiotics and intravenous hydration (with mannitol) are given
2. The patient is positioned in the supine position on a radiography table. The surgeon can stand on either side
3. Anaesthetic: general with endotracheal intubation. Nasogastric tube is passed
4. Skin preparation: the abdomen is cleansed with antiseptic (e.g. povidone-iodine, chlorhexidine) and draped up as for an upper abdominal incision
5. Access: a right Kocher's incision is made and muscles are divided by diathermy in the line of the incision
6. Examination and assessment
   - The gallbladder is examined for stones, thickening and adherence to surrounding structures
   - The pancreas, stomach, sigmoid colon, common bile duct and appendix are examined
7. Procedure
   - Calot's triangle is displayed by gentle traction on the liver upwards, on the stomach and duodenum downwards and on the gallbladder laterally
   - The cystic artery is ligated and divided
   - The peritoneal reflections between the fundus and the liver are divided
   - The cystic duct is identified and cannulated (to collect bile for microbiology and supply contrast medium for a cholangiogram). If the cholangiogram is normal the cystic duct is ligated and divided

1 cm from its junction with the common hepatic duct
- The gallbladder is removed and sent for histological examination
- Haemostasis is completed using diathermy coagulation
- A suction drain is placed in the subhepatic region if indicated

8. Closure in layers
9. Postoperative instructions
    - Measurement of drain output (the drain is usually removed at 48 hours)
    - The nasogastric tube is removed at about 18 hours

Q2
You use Kocher's incision. What other possible incisions can be used?

A2
1. Right upper paramedian
2. Right transverse (subcostal)
3. Upper midline

Q3
Give one practical difficulty you may encounter

A3
Occasionally, it is very difficult to separate the gallbladder from the liver.

Q4
What may cause this particular difficulty?

A4
There are two possible causes:
1. Fibrosis due to chronic inflammation
2. Malignancy, in which case the gallbladder, adjacent liver tissue and porta hepatis nodes should be sent for histology

Truncal Vagotomy and Pyloroplasty

Q1
How do you perform a truncal vagotomy? (Omit preoperative preparation and postoperative management)

A1
1. The patient is given a general anaesthetic with endotracheal intubation and placed in the supine position. A nasogastric tube is passed
2. The abdomen is prepared and draped as for an upper midline incision
3. An upper midline incision (about 18 cm long) skirting the umbilicus is made
4. A methodical assessment of the abdominal structures is carried out and other pathologies such as hiatus hernia and gallstones are looked for
5. The level of the hiatus is identified using the nasogastric tube as a guide with the assistant holding down the stomach
6. A 3–4 cm transverse incision is made through the peritoneum at the level of the hiatus. The phreno-oesophageal ligament is divided and the inferior phrenic vessels are avoided
7. The anterior vagal trunk is identified anterior to the gullet; it is separated from the gullet for about 5 cm upwards and downwards until its breakdown into hepatic and gastric branches and continuation as the anterior nerve of Latarget. The anterior trunk is clamped, divided and ligated as high as possible and at its point of breakdown. The resected segment is removed
8. The distal part of the oesophagus is encircled with the right thumb and index finger and its posterior mesentery is pushed to the right. The posterior vagal trunk is identified. It is separated from the oesophagus, crushed and cut as high as possible and below where it passes to the coeliac plexus and continues as the posterior nerve of Latarget. The resected segment is removed
9. Haemostasis is ensured
10. The hiatal incision is sutured transversely with interrupted non-absorbable sutures
11. Closure is *en masse* using looped nylon

Q2
In an obese patient the view may be inadequate. What additional manoeuvres do you use to improve the view?

A2
1. Excision of the xiphoid process
2. Tilting the operating table into a 25° head-up position
3. Mobilisation of the left lobe of the liver

Q3
How can you test for completeness of vagotomy?

A3
1. Hollander's insulin test
2. Burge's test, in which the residual vagal fibres are stimulated with an electrode-carrying clamp which encircles the oesophagus. The stimulation evokes gastric muscular contraction, which can be quantified
3. Grassi's test. A pH probe is placed in the stomach and the residual vagal fibres are stimulated in a manner similar to that in Burge's method

Q4
What adjunctive operation do you perform with truncal vagotomy in the treatment of a duodenal ulcer?

A4
I perform a Heineke–Mikulicz pyloroplasty.

Q5
What is the principle of this operation?

A5
The pyloroduodenal region is mobilised by Kocher's manoeuvre, and a 4 cm longitudinal incision is made over the pylorus (through all coats). The incision is then closed transversely.

Q6
What other adjunctive procedures can be carried out?

A6
1. Finney's pyloroplasty
2. Distal gastrectomy
3. Gastrojejunostomy

Repair of an Abdominal Aortic Aneurysm

Q1
How do you repair an abdominal aortic aneurysm?

A1
1. Preoperative preparation
   - Prophylactic antibacterial agents effective against staphylococci are commenced
   - The patient is catheterised
   - Venous and arterial lines are inserted
   - Investigations are reviewed, e.g. ultrasound, serum U+Es (urea and electrolytes), blood crossmatch, ECG (electrocardiogram), computed tomography
2. Anaesthetic is general with endotracheal intubation and epidural anaesthesia
3. The patient is positioned supine
4. Skin is prepared from nipples to mid-thighs and transparent adhesive tape is applied
5. Surgical access is achieved through a long midline incision skirting the umbilicus from xiphisternum to pubis
6. A methodical assessment of abdominal structures is carried out
7. Procedure
   - The bowel is displaced to the right upper quadrant and covered with moist packs. The sigmoid colon is also packed away
   - The posterior peritoneum is incised (anteriorly) to the right of the arcade supplying the left colon, and damage to the adjacent duodenum is avoided. The peritoneum is incised from the level of the left renal vein down to the common iliac arteries so that the abdominal aorta is well exposed
   - The common iliac arteries are then dissected out. The right artery usually adheres firmly to the left common iliac vein whereas the left artery is less adherent. Tapes are passed around the common iliac arteries
   - Depending on the extent of disease a suitable graft (woven Dacron) is selected. If the common iliac arteries are aneurysmal the distal limbs of the Y shaped graft may be anastomosed to the

common femoral arteries which can be exposed through the groins
- The patient is heparinised (5000 IU) and the iliac arteries are clamped first, then the aorta is clamped just distal to the renal arteries. Then the sac is incised and the contents evacuated. Bleeding from the lumbar, median sacral and inferior mesenteric arteries is controlled
- The Dacron prosthesis is trimmed to a suitable length and a sleeve is pulled over it
- The neck of the aneurysm is transfixed well below the clamp
- The upper anastomosis is made using 4/0 Prolene just distal to the renal arteries, and the sleeve is pulled over the suture line. Then a mitral clamp is applied below the sleeve and the upper clamp is released to test the anastomosis
- The distal ends of the graft are anastomosed to the cut ends of the common iliac arteries using a modified triangulation technique. If the common femoral arteries are used, a side-to-side anastomosis may be performed. The distal end may be sutured to the aorta
- The anaesthetist is warned when the clamps are removed to allow blood flow distally
- The sac is then debrided, trimmed and sutured over the graft using non-absorbable material
- The inferior mesenteric artery is reimplanted if the left colon looks ischaemic
- Closure is *en masse* using looped nylon
- A nasogastric tube is passed

Q2
What are the main complications of this operation?

A2
1. Haemorrhage due to anastomosis failure or heparinisation
2. Renal failure due to acute tubular necrosis or occlusion of renal arteries
3. Graft infection
4. Distal arterial occlusion
5. Paralytic ileus
6. Neurological deficit
7. Myocardial infarction

8. Graft occlusion
9. Pseudoaneurysm
10. Ischaemic colitis

Q3
How can you lessen the incidence of acute tubular necrosis?

A3
By decreasing the time of aortic clamping, ensuring adequate vascular volume and using drugs that increase renal blood flow such as dopamine $3 \mu g\, kg^{-1} min^{-1}$. Mannitol may also be used.

Q4
Why do you warn the anaesthetist when releasing the clamps?

A4
Because hypotension occurs owing to reduced distal peripheral resistance ensuing from the lack of oxygenated blood distally during clamping.

Q5
Does the closure of the aneurysm sac over the graft have any particular purpose?

A5
It reduces the incidence of aortoduodenal fistula and suture-line aneurysm.

Q6
What do you do if, 12 hours after the operation, the patient's left lower leg becomes pale, cold and pulseless?

A6
Having confirmed acute ischaemia on clinical grounds, I would perform a femoral embolectomy using a Fogarty catheter as soon as possible.

Burr Holes and Craniotomy

Q1
What are the stages of making a temporal burr hole? (Exclude preoperative preparation and postoperative management)

A1
1. The patient is given a general anaesthetic with endotracheal intubation and positioned supine with the head supported on a horseshoe-shaped head ring. Prophylactic antibiotics are administered (e.g. penicillin and flucloxacillin)
2. The completely shaven scalp is prepared with an antiseptic solution and the site of incision is marked. The incision should run vertically from just above the upper edge of the zygomatic bone at a point 2.5 cm anterior to the external auditory meatus. A 4 cm incision is made and the scalp is cut down to bone. The scalp is displaced from the bone using a periosteal elevator and its edges are held apart with a self-retaining retractor
3. A suitable perforator and burr are selected (of matching size and widest diameter)
4. Drilling is commenced using the perforator at 90° to the skull vault until the tip of the perforator just enters the inner table and a small area of dura is exposed
5. The conical burr is then used to expose a wide area of dura
6. One should be cautious when drilling near a fracture site as the bone may give way easily
7. Haemostasis is achieved using diathermy for bleeding from the dural surface and bone wax for bleeding from bone
8. If indicated, the dura can be opened in a cruciate fashion. Firstly, it is lifted up using a sharp hook and a small nick is made using a sharp pointed blade. Secondly, a dural guide is passed between the dura and brain and the dura is cut down to the guide in a cruciate fashion

Q2
If you find an extradural haematoma which cannot be evacuated through an exploratory temporal burr hole you have made following a head injury, how will you proceed?

A2
I will convert the burr hole to a craniectomy or craniotomy.

Q3
What are the main steps of a craniotomy? (Exclude preoperative preparation, anaesthesia and postoperative management)

A3
1. An inverted U-shaped scalp flap is made with its base towards the base of the skull. The sides of the flap should not overlie large venous sinuses and should be away from the midline by at least 2.5 cm. The scalp is cut down almost to the bone. Artery forceps are applied to the galea aponeurotica
2. The scalp flap is reflected backwards after sharply dissecting the subgaleal space composed of loose areolar tissue
3. The temporalis muscle and pericranium are cut by diathermy (along the sides of the flap) and scraped from the bone using a periosteal elevator
4. About five well spaced burr holes are made along the sides of the flap
5. The bone between burr holes is cut using a Gigli saw with its protective guide. The bone between the two basal burr holes is cut with bone cutters
6. The bone flap is hinged backwards with its attached pericranium and temporalis muscle, and the dura is sutured to the pericranium with interrupted hitch sutures at the edges of the bone defect
7. Haemostasis on the dural surface is ensured
8. If indicated, the dura is opened as a flap with its base towards the base of the skull

Haemorrhoidectomy

Q1
How do you carry out a haemorrhoidectomy?

A1
1. Preoperative preparation
   - The patient is given a disposable phosphate enema (128 ml)
   - The patient's blood should be grouped and saved
2. General anaesthetic and endotracheal intubation
3. The patient is positioned in the lithotomy position and the surgeon sits facing the perineum
4. The skin of the perineum and anus is prepared and Parke's proctoscope is passed per rectum
5. Procedure
   - A small haemostatic forceps is applied on the haemorrhoid and gently drawn towards the surgeon. A V-shaped incision is made in the anal skin at the base of the haemorrhoid. The haemorrhoid is then raised towards the lumen away from the internal sphincter fibres
   - The haemorrhoid is transfixed and ligated with an absorbable suture, then it is divided about 5 mm distal to the ligation and removed
   - The above procedure is repeated for other haemorrhoids but an attempt should be made to leave adequate mucocutaneous bridges otherwise an anal stricture will ensue
   - The anal canal is then packed with gauze or a sponge to keep the mucocutaneous bridges flat against the internal sphincter. A perineal pad and a firm T-bandage are then applied

Q2
Outline your postoperative management

A2
1. Daily laxatives, e.g. Fybogel and lactulose, are given
2. The dressings are removed
3. 50 mg of pethidine (intramuscular) may be required 30 minutes before bowel movements and change of dressing

4. External wounds may be managed with baths, irrigations and dressings
5. Gentle digital examination may be performed on the fifth day. If there is stenosis or spasm the anal dilator is used daily
6. Glycerine suppositories, enema or manual evacuation may be used for faecal retention

Q3
What postoperative complications may arise?

A3
1. Acute urinary retention
2. Reactionary haemorrhage
3. Constipation and faecal impaction (due to pain)
4. Anal stenosis
5. Faecal incontinence due to damage to the sphincter mechanism
6. Anal fissure
7. Recurrence of haemorrhoids
8. Perianal fistula formation

Q4
How is the internal sphincter distinguished from the external sphincter?

A4
The internal sphincter fibres look white whereas the external fibres look red.

Right Hemicolectomy

Q1
What operation would you perform for an operable carcinoma affecting the proximal part of the ascending colon?

A1
I would perform a right hemicolectomy.

Q2
Describe the procedure

A2
1. The patient (anaesthetised generally with endotracheal intubation) is positioned supine and the table is tilted 20° towards the operating surgeon who stands on the left
2. The whole abdomen is prepared from nipples to thighs
3. The abdominal cavity is entered through a long midline incision skirting the umbilicus
4. Soft bowel clamps are placed at 30 cm proximal to the ileocaecal valve and at the junction between the proximal and middle thirds of the transverse colon
5. The tumour is assessed (gently); the whole of the peritoneal cavity, para-aortic and mesenteric nodes, small and large bowel, liver and pelvis are also assessed
6. The caecum and ascending colon are mobilised medially
7. The parietal peritoneum is cut about 2 cm lateral to the ascending colon from the caecum to the hepatic flexure. The right colon is dissected from the posterior abdominal wall
8. The ileocolic artery and vein, the right colic artery and the right branch of the middle colic artery are identified, clamped, divided and ligated. These vessels should be divided close to their origin
9. Crushing bowel clamps are applied between the soft clamps about 1 cm from each end
10. The bowel is divided between the soft and crushing clamps and the specimen is removed and sent for histological examination. The right half of the greater omentum is also removed with the specimen
11. An ileocolic anastomosis is made (end to end) using a single

seromuscular layer of Vicryl sutures
12. The abdominal wall is closed *en masse*

Q3
Name three structures that should be identified and preserved in this operation

A3
1. Right ureter
2. Right gonadal vessels
3. Duodenum

Q4
Describe your technique for abdominal wall closure

A4
I usually perform an *en masse* closure using looped nylon (0/1). The bites are placed 1 cm away from each other and from the rectus sheath edge.

Q5
What are the main principles of intestinal anastomosis?

A5
The anastomosis should be between two viable bowel ends and tension free. It is usually performed using an inner (all coats) layer of continuous absorbable suture (e.g. chromic cat gut or Vicryl) on an eyeless needle. A second seromuscular layer of interrupted sutures (e.g. Vicryl or silk) may also be added to provide further security. The anastomosis should be air tight and fluid tight. It may be end-to-end, side-to-side, end-to-side or oblique, if the two intestinal ends are disproportionate in size. In colorectal anastomosis following anterior resection of the rectum, interrupted mattress sutures (e.g. PDS) are used. Alternatively, mechanical stapling devices can be used for intestinal anastomosis.

Laparoscopic Appendicectomy

Q1
Describe the procedure (only) of laparoscopic appendicectomy

A1

1. The patient also signs consent to an open procedure
2. Perioperative antibacterials are administered, e.g. cefuroxime and metronidazole
3. The patient is given general anaesthetic with endotracheal intubation
4. The whole abdomen is prepared
5. A Veress needle is inserted through a stab incision subumbilically, then a pneumoperitoneum is created using an insufflator which is set to deliver carbon dioxide. Once the pneumoperitoneum is created, the Veress needle is removed and replaced with a 10 mm cannula through which a diagnostic laparoscope attached to a video camera is passed and the diagnosis of appendicitis is confirmed
6. A second 5 mm cannula is inserted in the right hypochondrium below the costal margin, and blunt forceps are introduced through it to grasp the caecum and draw it towards the spleen. Then the operating table is tilted to displace the small bowel from the pelvis so that the ovaries can be examined. Any free fluid or pus is aspirated and sent for microbiological analysis
7. Once the diagnosis of appendicitis is confirmed a third 5 mm cannula is inserted low in the left iliac fossa under direct vision (the inferior epigastric vessels should be avoided)
8. The appendix is then grasped (with forceps introduced through the left iliac fossa cannula) and its mesentery is clearly displayed. The appendix is dissected from its mesentery as much as possible using hook diathermy introduced through the right hypochondrial port
9. A pre-tied catgut ligature is then introduced through the right hypochondrial 5 mm cannula down to the base of the appendix, which is ligated. A second pre-tied catgut ligature is introduced to ligate the appendix distal to the first ligature to avoid spillage of the luminal contents
10. The appendix is divided about 4 mm distal to the ligated base and held with forceps introduced through the right hypochondrial cannula
11. The laparoscope is removed from the 10 mm cannula, a 5 mm

laparoscope is introduced through the left 5 mm cannula, and the appendix is withdrawn through the 10 mm cannula

12. Peritoneal lavage using warm saline may be carried out
13. The pneumoperitoneum is released and the cannulas are removed
14. Wounds are infiltrated with 0.5% bupivacaine and closed with PDS for fascia and Steri-Strips for skin

Q2
Give one disadvantage of the procedure

A2
Prolonged operating time, especially when the procedure is carried out by less experienced trainees.

Q3
Do you attempt laparoscopic appendicectomy in all patients with suspected appendicitis?

A3
No. Male patients with classic clinical features of appendicitis should be treated with open appendicectomy. Laparoscopy is particularly useful in establishing the diagnosis in young females presenting with pain in the right iliac fossa. In such cases laparoscopic appendicectomy may be performed.

Laparoscopic Repair of Perforated Peptic Ulcer

Q1
How do you repair a perforated duodenal ulcer laparoscopically?

A1
1. Preoperative preparation
   - A nasogastric tube is passed
   - The patient is catheterised
   - An H_2-antagonist and a broad-spectrum antibacterial agent is administered intravenously
   - Investigations are reviewed, e.g. erect chest radiograph
   - The patient also signs consent for an open procedure
2. The anaesthetic is general with endotracheal intubation
3. The abdomen is prepared as for an open procedure
4. Procedure
   - A stab incision is made subumbilically and a Veress needle is introduced through which a pneumoperitoneum is created using carbon dioxide delivered from an insufflator set to deliver 2 litre/min initially for the first few litres then 5 litre/min
   - After the creation of the pneumoperitoneum the Veress needle is removed and an 11 mm cannula is introduced through which a diagnostic laparoscope attached to a video camera is passed. Laparoscopy is carried out in the reversed Trendelenburg position
   - Another 11 mm cannula is inserted just below the xiphisternum in the midline under laparoscopic vision. Two 5 mm cannulas are inserted in the right hypochondrium in the midclavicular and anterior axillary lines
   - The peritoneal cavity is irrigated with warm saline and the perforated ulcer is identified. The laparoscope is then moved to the upper 11 mm cannula
   - The lower 11 mm and lateral 5 mm cannulas are used for suturing and retraction
   - An endosuture (with the needle first) is introduced through the medial 5 mm portal. The needle is grasped with a needle holder introduced through the lower 11 mm cannula
   - The needle is passed through the duodenal wall, a small distance

77

away from the ulcer edge
- Using the left hand, an omental patch is mobilised and brought over the ulcer. The needle is then passed through the omental patch
- A 3 mm needle holder is passed through the medial 5 mm cannula to draw the needle out, then an extracorporeal Roeder knot is tied in the suture and pushed down to approximate firmly the omental patch over the ulcer. The same suture technique is repeated to insert as many sutures as necessary to close the ulcer
- Peritoneal lavage using warm saline is carried out at the end of the procedure for about 15 minutes. The fluid is then aspirated and the pneumoperitoneum is released
- The cannulas are removed and incisions are infiltrated with 0.5% bupivacaine and closed using polyamide sutures for fascia and nylon or Steri-Strips for skin

Q2
If the liver edge overlies the perforated ulcer so that you cannot visualise it, what will you do?

A2
I will pull the duodenum down or insert a fifth cannula level with the umbilicus (to the right) in the midclavicular line so that a retractor (held by an assistant) can be used to retract the liver edge.

Abdominoperineal Excision of the Rectum

Q1
What are the main indications for abdominoperineal excision of the rectum?

A1
1. Malignant tumours affecting the lower third of the rectum, particularly those of high-grade malignancy and/or locally advanced and fixed
2. Malignant tumours affecting the anal canal that fail to resolve with chemotherapy and radiotherapy

Q2
What histological types of malignant tumour could involve the anal canal?

A2
1. Squamous cell carcinoma
2. Adenocarcinoma
3. Basal cell carcinoma
4. Melanoma
5. Kaposi's sarcoma

Q3
What does the excised specimen of abdominoperineal excision of the rectum usually contain?

A3
1. The sigmoid colon
2. The rectum and mesorectum
3. The anal canal
4. The anus and perineal skin

Q4
What are the anatomical markings for the perineal incision anteriorly and posteriorly?

A4
Anteriorly:
1. Male patient: midpoint between the anus and the bulb of the urethra
2. Female patient: the posterior vaginal wall is included in the specimen up to the posterior fornix

Posteriorly:
3. The sacrococcygeal articulation

Q5
In the male patient, does the anterior (perineal) plane of dissection go anterior or posterior to the transverse perineal muscles, and why?

A5
The dissection plane should lie posterior to the transverse perineal muscles to avoid damaging the urethra.

Q6
Describe two practical difficulties you may encounter in this procedure

A6
1. Extensive pelvic oozing (perineal)
2. Herniation of small bowel through the pelvic floor

Q7
How would you manage these two problems?

A7
1. The oozing can be managed with gauze packing for 24–48 hours
2. The herniation of small bowel can be prevented by placing a plastic bag in the pelvic floor for approximately 48 hours

Thyroidectomy

Q1
A 50-year-old woman presents with a 2 cm lump in the right hemithyroid. What investigations would you perform?

A1
1. Fine-needle aspiration cytology (FNAC)
2. Ultrasound scan
3. Thyroid function tests and autoantibodies
4. Radioisotope scan

Q2
FNAC suggests a follicular neoplasm, ultrasound confirms the presence of a solid lump and the radioisotope scan shows a cold nodule. How would you manage such a patient?

A2
I would perform a right hemithyroidectomy to exclude malignancy.

Q3
Describe the procedure of hemithyroidectomy

A3
1. The anaesthetic is general with endotracheal intubation (oral or nasal route)
2. The patient is positioned supine (with a head-up tilt of 15°). The head rests on a ring and a sandbag is placed in the interscapular region
3. The neck is prepared and draped
4. A transverse collar incision is made approximately finger breadth above the suprasternal notch. The skin and platysma are divided
5. The superior and inferior subplatysmal flaps are raised. The superior flap should extend to the thyroid cartilage, and the inferior flap should reach the sternum. A Joll's retractor is then applied
6. The cervical fascia is divided in the midline and the strap muscles are retracted laterally
7. The inferior and middle thyroid veins are ligated and divided. The

inferior thyroid artery is identified and ligated in continuity as proximal as possible. The recurrent laryngeal nerve is identified in the groove between the trachea and the oesophagus and in relation to the inferior thyroid artery. The nerve is traced upwards where it enters the larynx. The nerve should be protected from injury and use if diathermy close to the nerve is avoided

8. The superior thyroid vascular pedicle is ligated and divided, then the thyroid lobe is completely mobilised and excised. The isthmus is oversewn with absorbable sutures. Haemostasis is completed and a section drain is placed in the subfascial space. The fascia is closed in the midline with absorbable sutures, then the platysma and skin are closed. Examination of the contralateral thyroid lobe and preservation of the parathyroid glands (if possible) are part of the procedure

Q4
Describe the arterial blood supply of the thyroid gland

A4
The superior thyroid artery, a branch of the external carotid artery, supplies the upper pole. The inferior thyroid artery, a branch of the thyrocervical trunk, supplies the lower pole. The thyrocervical artery arises from the subclavian artery. An accessory thyroid gland occasionally arises from the aortic arch and connects to the thyroid isthmus inferiorly.

Q5
What are the main complications of this procedure?

A5
1. Haematoma, which could precipitate respiratory obstruction
2. Wound infection
3. Recurrent laryngeal nerve palsy
4. Superior laryngeal nerve palsy
5. Hypothyroidism
6. Hypoparathyroidism
7. Keloid scar
8. Stitch granuloma

Below-knee Amputation

Q1
Give six contraindications to below-knee amputation

A1
1. Joint contractures affecting the knee or hip joints
2. Severe osteoarthritis of the knee
3. Spasticity or paralysis of the lower limb due to previous cerebrovascular accident (CVA)
4. Sensory neuropathy affecting the skin of the future stump
5. Infection of the lower limb requiring a higher amputation
6. Ischaemia of the lower leg requiring a higher amputation

Q2
What are the main steps of the below-knee amputation procedure

A2
1. The anaesthetic may be general, epidural or spinal. Intravenous antibiotics including penicillin are administered
2. The patient may be positioned prone or supine
3. The lines of incision are marked. A long posterior myocutaneous flap is most commonly used
4. The anterior incision is made down to the tibia; the anterior tibial neurovascular structures are ligated and divided. The lateral incisions are then made and common peroneal neurovascular structures are ligated and divided. The tibia is resected (after elevating the periosteum) 1–2 cm proximal to the skin incision using a Gigli saw at a 45° angle. The fibula is resected 1 cm proximal to the tibial level. The posterior tibial neurovascular structures are ligated and divided, and a myocutaneous flap (skin plus the gastrocnemius and soleus muscle) is created. The flap is tapered and rotated anteriorly to cover the tibial stump, which should be made smooth using a file.
5. The muscles may be sutured to the tibial periosteum (myoplasty) and the fascia is closed with Vicryl. Prior to closure the wound is irrigated with normal saline and a subfascial suction drain is inserted. The haemostasis should be meticulous. The skin is then closed with

interrupted nylon and a rigid dressing is applied.

Q3
What are the basic principles of marking the skin flaps if one uses a long posterior flap?

A3
1. The level of tibial resection is selected. It should be 1 in away from the knee joint for every 30 cm (1 ft) of the patient's height. The absolute minimum distance is 7 cm from the tibial tuberosity
2. The anterior incision lies 1 cm distal to the level of the tibial resection and extends two thirds of the entire circumference of the lower leg at the level of bone resection
3. The lateral incisions extend distally and their length is approximately half that of the anterior incision

Q4
What other flaps can be used?

A4
1. Skewed flaps
2. Equal anterior and posterior flaps

Q5
What preoperative investigations can predict the healing rate of the below-knee stump?

A5
1. Doppler pressure of the calf
2. Doppler pressure of the thigh
3. Xenon-133 blood flow measurement of the skin
4. Transcutaneous PaO_2 of the skin
5. Fibre-optic fluorimetry

Splenectomy

Q1
How would you perform a splenectomy?

A1
1. Preoperative preparation
   - When trauma is the indication it is essential that the patient is adequately resuscitated before surgery
   - Investigations are checked, FBC (full blood count), plain radiographs (looking for fractures of lower ribs), clotting screen and peritoneal lavage. Crossmatched blood should be available
   - Broad-spectrum antibiotics prophylaxis, e.g. cefuroxime and metronidazole
   - Correction of any preoperative cytopenia or coagulopathy
2. Anaesthetic is general with endotracheal intubation
3. Position of the patient is supine
4. Skin preparation and drapes are as for an upper abdominal incision
5. Access is via a left subcostal incision. Other suitable incisions include upper midline and left paramedian incisions
6. The liver and lymph nodes are assessed and a search for spleniculi is made
7. Procedure
   - The lesser sac is entered through an opening in the greater omentum made by dividing about 9 cm of the omentum
   - The splenic artery is ligated at the upper border of the pancreas
   - The spleen is drawn medially by the left hand
   - The left leaf of the lienorenal ligament is incised
   - The spleen is mobilised forwards and medially by gently dissecting it from the tail of the panaceas, left colic flexure and diaphragm
   - The gastrosplenic ligament is incised and the short gastric vessels divided
   - The splenic artery and vein are identified at the hilum, doubly clamped, ligated and divided
   - The right leaf of the lienorenal ligament is incised and the spleen is removed
8. Closure
   - Haemostasis is ensured

- The pedical ligatures are checked
- A suction drain is placed in the splenic bed
- Closure is in layers
9. Postoperative care
   - Full blood count after the operation
   - Long-term antibiotic prophylaxis is given, e.g. penicillin 250 mg daily
   - Polypneumococcal vaccine (Pneumovax) is administered

Q2
What are the complications of this operation?

A2
1. Haemorrhage
2. Postsplenectomy sepsis (especially pneumococci). All age groups are susceptible
3. Subphrenic abscess and wound infection
4. Thrombocythaemia and leukocytosis. Aspirin (300 mg daily) should be commenced if the platelet count exceeds 750×10^9 per litre
5. Inadvertent damage to the tail of the pancreas and stomach during surgery
6. Acute gastric dilatation
7. Ischaemic perforation of the greater curvature of the stomach
8. Pancreatic fistula
9. Gastric fistula
10. Pulmonary atelectasis
11. Pancreatitis

Q3
Would your operation be different if the indications were traumatic splenic injury?

A3
Yes
1. The left subcostal incision is unsuitable and an upper midline incision is more appropriate to assess other abdominal structures
2. Priority is given to control of bleeding as quickly as possible by mobilising the spleen into the wound and controlling the vascular

pedicle
3. An attempt should be made to preserve as much splenic tissue as possible. Any spleniculi are not removed. Splenic pulp may be scattered in the splenic bed to encourage splenosis

Q4
What are the indications for draining the splenic bed?

A4
1. Inadequate haemostasis
2. Damage to the tail of the pancreas
3. Contamination of the bed with gastrointestinal contents

Q5
What are the main functions of the spleen?

A5
1. Filtering functions include removal of old and abnormal red blood cells, white cells and platelets and cellular debris
2. Immunological functions include opsonin production, antibody synthesis and protection from infection
3. There is also a storage function. Approximately 35% of the body's platelets are stored in the spleen

Open Appendicectomy

Q1
What are the steps in an appendicectomy?

A1
1. Preoperative preparation
   - Antibiotic prophylaxis with metronidazole 1 g per rectum is started
   - Correction of dehydration, and broad-spectrum antibiotics (cefuroxime and metronidazole) if there is generalised peritonitis
2. Anaesthetic is general with endotracheal intubation
3. The position of the patient is supine
4. Skin preparation and drapes
5. Incision
   - A Lanz incision is made passing through McBurney's point to end just medial to the linea semilunaris
   - Subcutaneous fat, Scarpa's fascia and underlying areolar tissue are divided
   - The external oblique is split in the direction of its fibres and retracted
   - The internal oblique and transversus abdominis are split using Mayo's straight scissors
   - The parietal peritoneum is picked up by a pair of dissecting forceps and a hole is made in it which is enlarged using scissors
   - The caecum is pushed into the wound
   - The appendix is mobilised by blunt dissection with the fingers
   - The mesoappendix is clamped and ligated with 1/0 chromic catgut or Vicryl
   - The base of the appendix is crushed with a haemostat and ligated (proximal to the haemostat). The appendix is cut just distal to the haemostat and removed
   - A scromuscular purse string is inserted into the caecum. The ligated appendix stump is invaginated while the purse string is tied
   - Peritoneal lavage is carried out
6. Closure
   - Haemostasis is ensured
   - A drain is not usually required
   - Closure is in layers using Vicryl

7. Postoperative care
   - Continue antibiotics if there is peritonitis
   - Free fluids are usually commenced 24 hours later
   - The histology report is checked

Q2
If you find that the appendix is not macroscopically inflamed, what should you look for?

A2
1. Terminal ileitis, which may be due to tuberculosis, Crohn's disease or *Yersinia* infection
2. Diverticular inflammation or tumour of the large bowel
3. Meckel's diverticulitis
4. Other organs such as liver, kidney, gallbladder, duodenum, ovaries, uterine tubes and uterus are examined. The incision may need to be enlarged

Q3
How do you manage an appendix mass?

A3
An ultrasound examination is performed. If no pus is seen, the mass is managed conservatively with broad-spectrum antimicrobials (e.g. metronidazole and cefuroxime). The surface markings of the mass are observed daily to monitor response. If pus is observed on ultrasound examination, it should be drained (e.g. percutaneously under ultrasound guidance) and antibiotics should be commenced. The possibility of a perforated caecal neoplasm should be considered.

Carpal Tunnel Syndrome

Q1
What are the causes of carpal tunnel syndrome?

A1
Recognised causes include:
1. Rheumatoid arthritis
2. Myxoedema
3. Osteoarthritis of the wrist
4. Diabetes mellitus
5. Previous fracture of the lower end of the radius
6. Acromegaly
7. Pregnancy
8. Idiopathic cases are common

Q2
How would you perform a surgical decompression of the median nerve in carpal tunnel syndrome?

A2
1. Preoperative preparation
   - Conduct electrophysiological studies of the median nerve
   - Mark the side
   - Test for sickle cell anaemia in Afro-Caribbean patients
2. Anaesthetic
   - Local anaesthetic may be used – local infiltration or Bier's block
   - General anaesthetic may also be used
3. Position of the patient is supine with the arm extended on a side table
4. Skin preparation
   - The arm is exsanguinated, then a pneumatic tourniquet is applied and inflated to 250 mmHg. The time is noted
   - The lower half of the forearm is draped so that the distal part of it and the hand remain exposed
5. Incision
   - A longitudinal incision is made from the distal flexor crease and extended distally for about 5 cm in line with the ulnar aspect of

the third digit
- The flexor retinaculum is then exposed. A MacDonald's instrument is placed under the retinaculum, which is then incised longitudinally down to the MacDonald's instrument. The median nerve is seen in the incised tunnel

6. Closure
- The tourniquet is deflated and haemostasis is ensured
- The skin is closed with interrupted nylon sutures
- Compression bandaging is applied

7. Postoperative care
- The compression dressing is replaced by an adhesive dressing 24 hours later
- Elevation of the hand is recommended
- Early exercise of the fingers is encouraged
- Sutures are removed in 10 days

Q3
In rheumatoid patients with a hypertrophic synovium, what additional procedure would you consider?

A3
Flexor tendon synovectomy.

Q4
What branches of the median nerve could be damaged?

A4
1. The motor branch to the thenar muscles
2. The palmar cutaneous branch

Q5
Is there an alternative surgical approach to treatment?

A5
Yes. Carpal tunnel syndrome has recently been treated with endoscopic release using the two-portal technique.

Q6
What are the main advantages of this procedure?

A6
1. Minimal scarring
2. Lower incidence of wound complications
3. Earlier return to work

Gastrectomy

Q1
What is the standard operation for localised distal carcinoma of the stomach?

A1
A radical abdominal subtotal gastrectomy (R2).

Q2
Describe the procedure

A2
1. The anaesthetic is general with endotracheal intubation. The position is supine. The whole abdomen is prepared and draped appropriately
2. Laparotomy is performed through a long midline incision
3. A thorough assessment of the intra-abdominal contents is carried out to assess the extent of disease. Ascites, liver metastases, involved nodes and deep deposits in the greater omentum are particularly searched for
4. The greater omentum is lifted and dissected off the mesocolon through the bloodless plane. The greater omentum is peeled off up to the superior pancreatic border
5. The left gastroepiploic vessels, at the left extremity of the greater omentum, are ligated and divided after dissecting the lymph nodes at the origin of the artery
6. At the right extremity of the greater omentum, the subpyloric lymph nodes at the origin of the right gastroepiploic artery are dissected and then the vessels are ligated and divided
7. The anterior leaf of the lesser omentum is incised above the pylorus to dissect the suprapyloric lymph nodes and to ligate and divide the right gastric artery
8. Kocher's mobilisation of the duodenum is performed. The duodenum is then transected 4 cm distal to the pylorus, and the distal end is cut and closed with two layers of Vicryl
9. The lymph nodes and peritoneum are dissected off the hepatic artery
10. The nodes at the origin of the left gastric artery are dissected, then the

artery is ligated and divided

11. The structures along the lesser curve are dissected off down to the level of resection
12. The proximal stomach is transected between two clamps. The level of transection should be 6 cm proximal to the tumour
13. A loop of proximal jejunum is drawn up. The afferent loop should be as short as possible. The anastomosis (antecolic) between the proximal stomach remnant and the jejunal loop is made using a combined linear stapling and cutting device

Q3
What do you mean by R2 gastrectomy?

A3
This refers to gastrectomy that includes N1 and N2 lymph nodes. N1 nodes are located within 3 cm of the primary tumour. The next nodes to be affected are N2 nodes, which include the right paracardial, left gastric, common hepatic and coeliac lymph nodes in this example.

Q4
What operation would you perform for an operable carcinoma of the cardia?

A4
I would perform a radical total gastrectomy through a left thoraco-abdominal incision.

Q5
Briefly describe the arterial blood supply of the stomach

A5
The lesser curve is supplied by the right gastric artery, a branch of the common hepatic artery and the left gastric artery, a branch of the coeliac axis. The greater curvature is supplied by the right gastroepiploic artery, a branch of the gastroduodenal artery, a branch of the splenic artery. The fundus is supplied by the vasa brevia arising from the splenic or gastroepiploic arteries.

SECTION 2

Applied Physiology and Critical Care

Respiratory System

Q1
What are the adverse effects of intermittent positive pressure ventilation with positive end expiratory pressure (PEEP)?

A1
The respiratory changes include maldistribution of inspired gases, collapse of distal pulmonary units, damage to the alveolar–capillary barrier, barotrauma, bronchopulmonary dysplasia, bronchiolectasis, pneumonia and decreased surfactant activity. The barotrauma effects include subpleural blebs of air, pneumothorax, pneumomediastinum and subcutaneous emphysema.

Q2
What is 'surfactant'?

A2
Surfactant is a phospholipid (predominantly dipalmitoyl phosphatidylcholine) secreted as lamellar bodies by type II alveolar cells. It reduces surface tension and helps to minimise the tendency for alveoli to collapse.

Q3
What are the cardiovascular consequences of intermittent positive pressure ventilation (IPPV)?

A3
IPPV reduces venous return and increases pulmonary vascular resistance, thus causing a reduction in cardiac output. In patients with cardiac failure, a paradoxical rise in cardiac output and blood pressure occurs. This may be due to correction of hypoxia, a decrease in oxygen consumption and a reduction in the afterload.

Q4
What is the normal distribution of ventilation and perfusion in

the human lung? How is this affected by mechanical ventilation?

A4

Ventilation increases from the upper to the lower regions of the lung. Blood flow also increases downwards but does so to a greater extent than ventilation. This creates three zones in the lung, an upper zone with ventilation:perfusion $(V:Q)$ ratio > 1, a middle zone with a $V:Q$ ratio almost equal 1 and a lower zone with a $V:Q$ ratio < 1. The overall $V:Q$ ratio in a healthy person is 0.8. IPPV causes a more evenly distributed ventilation with an increase in the $V:Q$ ratio.

Q5
Give five complications of endotracheal intubation

A5
1. Intubation of a single bronchus
2. Intubation of the oesophagus
3. Tube migration
4. Obstruction
5. Mucosal oedema, ulceration, scar formation and stenosis of the trachea

Shock

Q1
What does endotoxin consist of?

A1
It consists of a lipid moiety (lipid A), a core polysaccharide and oligosaccharide side chains.

Q2
What is the pathophysiology of endotoxic shock?

A2
The lipopolysaccharide–lipopolysaccharide binding protein (LPS–LBP) complex stimulates the CD14 receptors on macrophages causing the release of tumour necrosis factor (TNF) and interleukin-1 (IL-1). The two cytokines stimulate cyclo-oxygenase, platelet activating factor (PAF) and nitric oxide synthase; IL-6 and IL-8 also appear in the circulation. Cyclo-oxygenase produces three prostaglandins, each of which has a distinct physiological effect. PAF causes platelet aggregation, increased vascular permeability and hypotension. Nitric oxide (NO) produces vasodilatation and inhibition of platelet aggregation. Endothelin also causes the release of lysosomal enzymes, which produce vasoactive kinins. Kinins can cause vasodilatation, increased vascular permeability, myocardial depression and activation of clotting mechanisms. Other effects of endotoxin include stimulation of Hageman factor (clotting cascade) and the alternative complement pathway. These pathophysiological mechanisms are responsible for the clinical manifestations of endotoxic shock: hypotension, pyrexia, renal failure, DIC (disseminated intravascular coagulation), etc.

Q3
Describe the sympathoadrenal and neuroendocrine responses to shock

A3
Hypotension and decreased blood flow stimulate chemoreceptors and

baroreceptors, causing increased sympathetic nervous activity and noradrenaline release. Hypovolaemia also stimulates the adrenal medulla to release adrenaline and noradrenaline. Catecholamines and sympathetic stimulation cause tachycardia, increased systemic resistance, increased myocardial contractility and decreased venous capacitance, thus raising cardiac output and blood pressure; renal hypoperfusion increases renin output by the juxtoglomerular cells. Renin converts angiotensinogen into angiotensin I. The latter is converted into angiotensin II and III by the converting enzyme and aminopeptidase, respectively. Angiotensin II and III cause vasoconstriction and aldosterone release. Aldosterone leads to sodium and water retention. The neuroendocrine response consists of increased secretion of ACTH (adrenocorticotrophic hormone), ADH (antidiuretic hormone), growth hormone and endogenous opioid peptides.

Q4
Describe the mechanism of reperfusion injury

A4
During ischaemia, xanthine dehydrogenase is converted to xanthine oxidase, and ATP is converted to hypoxanthine. When oxygen again becomes available, xanthine oxidase converts hypoxanthine into uric acid, thus generating free radicals, e.g. O_2^-. These free radicals are toxic and cause tissue injury. Gastrointestinal mucosa is particularly vulnerable to reperfusion injury.

Q5
Define shock

A5
This is a state of inadequate organ perfusion/tissue oxygenation.

Q6
Name four causes of shock

A6
Four causes are (1) hypovolaemia, (2) sepsis, (3) cardiogenic and (4) anaphylaxis.

Q7
What is the commonest cause of shock in a trauma patient?

A7
Haemorrhagic.

Q8
Describe the different classes of haemorrhage and the likely clinical associated findings.

A8
Class 1 - Upto 15% blood loss - Pulse<100, BP normal, RR=14 - 20, Urine output >30mls/hr.
Class 2 - 15 to 30% blood loss - Pulse>100, BP normal, RR=20 - 30, Urine output 20 - 30mls/hr.
Class 3 - 30to 40% blood loss - Pulse>120, BP decreased, RR=30 - 40, Urine output 5 - 15mls/hr.
Class 4 - >40% blood loss - Pulse>140, BP decreased, RR>35, Urine output negligible.

Q9
What sort of responses can shocked patients have to initial fluid resuscitation?

A9
The responses to initial fluid resuscitation can be broken down into 1)Rapid response where the vital signs return to normal and stay normal, 2) Transient response where the vital signs transiently improve but then return to being abnormal and 3) No response where the vital signs remain abnormal. This response has a bearing on the requirement for subsequent therapies.

Q10
Define blood pressure.

A10
Blood pressure is the pressure in the vascular system due to blood flow. It has a maximum (systolic), a minimum (diastolic) and a mean (diastolic +

1/3[systolic-diastolic]).

Q12
What is the equation relating blood pressure to cardiac output and systemic vascular resistance?

A12
Mean arterial pressure - Right atrial pressure = cardiac output * systemic vascular resistance.

Q13
Name two devices that can be used to derive cardiac output.

A13
Oesophageal doppler and a Swan-Ganz catheter. They use the principles of doppler and thermodilution respectively.

Q14
What other parameters can be measured or derived using a Swan-Ganz catheter?

A14
Other parameters include the pulmonary artery wedge pressure, systemic vascular resistance, pulmonary vascular resistance and cardiac stroke volume (remember cardiac output = heart rate × stroke volume).

Q15
Name some of the complications of a Swan-Ganz catheter.

A15
These include Dysrrhythmias, pulmonary embolus, pulmonary infarction, pulmonary artery rupture, infection, haematoma and thrombosis at site of insertion.

Q16
Draw an arterial line circuit.

A16
Cannula----flush device----pressure bag system----transducer----monitor.

Thoracic Trauma

Q1
What are the principles of managing a patient with thoracic trauma?

A1
1. A detailed history is obtained
2. Primary survey is carried out. Airway, breathing and circulation are assessed and adequately established, with airway and breathing being the highest priorities. Vascular access is established
3. The neurological status and Glasgow Coma Score are determined

Q2
What are the most common causes of asphyxia in trauma patients?

A2
1. Inadequate airway
2. Chest injury:
   - Tension pneumothorax
   - Open pneumothorax
   - Flail chest

Q3
Describe the management of the airway

A3
1. The mouth is opened and the tip of the tongue is pulled forward. The angles of the mandible are pulled forward
2. The mouth and pharynx are suctioned to clear blood, mucus, vomitus and foreign bodies. An oral airway may be introduced
3. Orotracheal intubation is performed if indicated. Stabilisation of the cervical spine is ensured, with a second person applying axial traction during the intubation, unless a lateral cervical spine radiograph has already been taken and shows no abnormality.
4. If ventilation failure starts developing and orotracheal intubation is

not possible, cricothyroidotomy is performed; this is to be preferred to tracheostomy in an emergency

Q4
How would you perform a cricothyroidotomy? What does ATLS suggest in the case of a child?

A4
The patient is positioned supine with the neck extended. A stab incision is made through the cricothyroid membrane using a scalpel. Once the scalpel enters the airway, a curved metal tube is inserted. The cricothyroid membrane lies between the cricoid and thyroid cartilages. Alternatively, a large-bore cannula and needle are introduced percutaneously through the cricothyroid membrane. A surgical cricothyroidotomy is not recommended in a child of less than 12 years owing to the risk of damage to the cricoid cartilage.

Q5
What are the principles of management of flail chest?

A5
1. Airway obstruction and the haemopneumothorax are managed immediately
2. Early stabilisation of the flail segment is achieved, with firm support
3. Conservative management without mechanical ventilation is applied if the PaO_2 is above 8 kPa, the $PaCO_2$ is below 8 kPa and the respiratory rate is below 35/min.
4. Mechanical ventilation is indicated if:
   - PaO_2 < 8 kPa, $PaCO_2$ > 8 kPa and respiratory rate > 35/min
   - The patient is severely shocked
   - General anaesthesia is required
   - Pre-existing lung disease is present

The patient is kept on intensive care for 2–5 days and returned to the ward when the pain is well controlled and the cough is effective.

5. Pain is controlled with epidural anaesthesia, intercostal nerve block, opiates, etc
6. Chest physiotherapy is arranged to coincide with periods of maximal

relief
7. Sputum is sent for microbiological analysis, and infections are treated with the appropriate antimicrobials

Q6
Consider the chest radiograph in Figure 1. What are the abnormal findings?

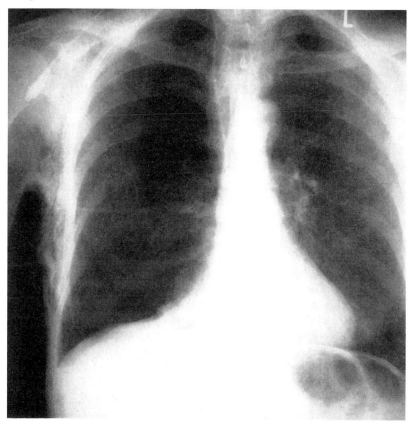

Figure 1

A6
1. Right-sided pneumothorax
2. Central venous catheter through the right subclavian vein

3. Right pleural catheter *in situ*
4. Surgical emphysema

Q7
In the presence of traumatic haemothorax, what are the indications for thoracotomy?

A7
1. Bleeding rate > 100–200 ml/h
2. Total haemorrhagic output > 1500 ml

Q8
What is the usual source of the haemorrhage in such circumstances?

A8
The chest wall accounts for 75–80% of cases.

Q9
Describe the procedure of inserting a chest drain for a haemopneumothorax

A9
1. The chest radiograph is examined
2. The conscious patient is positioned sitting up and leaning forward
3. The site of drain insertion is selected, between the midaxillary and anterior axillary lines, and between the fourth and seventh intercostal spaces
4. 1% lignocaine (approximately 10 ml) is infiltrated through the skin and periosteum along the upper border of the rib at the chosen interspace. The pleura should also be infiltrated
5. A short transverse incision (1.5–2 cm) is made. The scalpel should find the rib below the intercostal space to be breached. The remainder of the track is completed through the interspace to the pleural cavity using artery forceps
6. A 28 Fr Argyl drain is inserted into the pleural cavity through the track. The drain is sutured in position using silk or Prolene and a pursestring suture is applied. The drain is connected to an underwater seal drainage bottle.

Q10
Describe briefly the procedure of anterolateral thoracotomy

A10

1. The patient is positioned obliquely with the ipsilateral hip and shoulder supported on sandbags
2. An incision is made along the appropriate rib (usually the fifth) starting near the midline and extending to the axilla 2.5 cm below the angle of the scapula
3. The upper rectus abdominis, the serratus anterior and the pectoralis major muscles are divided along the incision. The periosteum is also divided along the incision and stripped from the rib. A cutting diathermy point is usually used. The ribs are separated using a rib spreader
4. The pleura is opened. The pericardium may be opened (if indicated) anterior to the phrenic nerve

Acute Pancreatitis

Q1
What are the causes of acute pancreatitis?

A1
The causes include
1. Gallstones (accounts for 40% of cases)
2. Alcohol (accounts for 40% of cases)
3. Hypercalcaemia
4. Hyperlipidaemia
5. Familial inheritance
6. Protein deficiency
7. Iatrogenic, e.g. ERCP (endoscopic retrograde cholangio-pancreatography), pancreatic biopsy, gastric surgery
8. Drugs such as corticosteroids, thiazide, diuretics, oestrogens and azathioprine
9. Pancreas divisum
10. Trauma

Q2
Outline the pathophysiology of acute pancreatitis and its systemic manifestations

A2
Initially, there is intracellular activation of digestive enzymes and autodigestion of the pancreas triggered by several factors, e.g. gallstones, alcohol, hyperlipidaemia. This leads to a local inflammatory process. The inflamed acinar cells and invading leukocytes produce powerful cytokines, especially interleukin-1 (IL-1) and tumour necrosis factor alpha (TNF-α). These cytokines mediate the systemic inflammatory response syndrome (SIRS) by stimulating the production of nitric oxide, IL-8, IL-6, platelet activating factor and IL-10, and the release of oxygen-free radicals and inflammatory enzymes. This cascade of events results in the systemic manifestations, which include tachycardia, fever, hypotension, ARDS (acute respiratory distress syndrome), acute tubular necrosis and vascular leakage.

Q3

What are the principles of management of acute pancreatitis?

A3

1. Oral intake is withheld and a nasogastric tube is passed
2. Intravenous fluid replacement
3. Oxygen therapy if $PaO_2 < 70\,mmHg$
4. Correction of serum calcium and magnesium
5. Broad-spectrum antibiotics in severe cases
6. Intravenous H_2-antagonists
7. Peritoneal lavage if severe pancreatitis does not improve after 48 hours of standard treatment
8. Total parenteral nutrition if a severely ill patient is unable to eat for more than a week
9. Endoscopic sphincterotomy for biliary pancreatitis if the stone is lodged in the ampulla of Vater
10. Surgery for severe necrotising pancreatitis: dead and infected tissue is removed. In biliary cases, cholecystectomy. Two large drains may be inserted for postoperative lavage

Q4
When do you suspect necrotising pancreatitis clinically?

A4

1. If more than three of Ranson's criteria are present
2. Contrast-enhanced CT (computed tomography) scan may show necrotic and oedematous tissue
3. Percutaneous needle aspiration may reveal bacteria and necrotic debris

Q5
What are Ranson's criteria?

A5

Ranson's criteria determine the severity of acute pancreatitis:

1. Criteria present initially include age > 55 years, WBC (white blood cell count) > 1600/µl, blood glucose > 200 mg/dl, serum LDH (lactate dehydrogenase) > 350 IU/l and AST (aspartate aminotransferase) > 250 IU/dl

2. Criteria developing during the first 48 hours include haematocrit fall by > 10%, BUN (blood urea nitrogen) > 8 mg/dl, serum Ca^{2+} < 8 mg/dl, arterial PaO_2 < 60 mmHg, base deficit > 4 mEq/l and fluid sequestration > 6000 ml

Q6
What is the main treatment for a pancreatic pseudocyst?

A6
1. Small asymptomatic cysts usually resolve spontaneously
2. Mature cysts can be drained into the stomach or jejunum
3. Immature cysts causing symptoms can be drained percutaneously under imaging (ultrasound or CT) guidance
4. Occasionally small cysts can be excised

Postoperative Respiratory Complications

Q1
What is the commonest postoperative respiratory complication?

A1
Atelectasis. It affects 25% of patients who have had abdominal surgery.

Q2
How does it present?

A2
It presents with pyrexia, tachypnoea and tachycardia. It accounts for approximately 90% of febrile episodes in the first 48 hours.

Q3
How is it treated?

A3
1. Clearing the airway (coughing, nasotracheal suction and/or chest percussion)
2. Humidified oxygen
3. Bronchodilators and mucolytic agents may be used
4. Antimicrobials if there is superadded infection (if atelectasis lasts more than 72 hours)

Q4
What can be done to prevent this complication?

A4
1. Early mobilisation
2. Encouragement to cough
3. Breathing exercises (preoperative teaching)
4. Frequent changes in position
5. Cessation of smoking before surgery
6. Loss of weight before surgery
7. Adequate analgesia (e.g. epidural anaesthetic for laparotomies)

Q5
What laboratory findings do you expect in a patient with pulmonary embolism?

A5
1. Hypoxaemia
2. Elevated LDH (lactate dehydrogenase)
3. Wedge-shaped peripheral infiltrate with or without pleural effusion on the chest radiograph .
4. Ventilation–perfusion mismatch on V/Q scan (reduced perfusion and normal ventilation)
5. Obstruction or filling defect on pulmonary angiogram
6. T-wave inversion and ST elevation on the electrocardiogram (present in 15% of cases)

Q6
What is the role of surgery in the management of pulmonary thromboembolism?

A6
1. Thoracotomy and pulmonary embolectomy are indicated for massive pulmonary embolism, particularly if there is refractory hypotension despite maximal resuscitation, or anticoagulation is contraindicated. Cardiopulmonary bypass is required
2. Transvenous suction catheters may be used to remove emboli (Greenfield catheters)
3. Venous thrombectomy (iliac or femoral) for recurrent embolism. Greenfield's filter may be inserted under radiological control to achieve the same aim

Q7
What is ARDS?

A7
This is acute respiratory distress syndrome which is a non-cardiogenic pulmonary oedema.

Q8
List some of the features of ARDS.

A8
ARDS is a clinical syndrome of
1. Refractory hypoxaemia
2. Pulmonary wedge pressure < 18
3. Stiff non compliant lungs
4. Respiratory distress
5. Diffuse pulmonary infiltrates.

Q9
Name six causes of ARDS.

A9
Trauma, burns, sepsis, pancreatitis, disseminated carcinomatosis, fat embolism.

Q10
What is the mortality associated with ARDS.

A10
This is between 40 and 60%.

Q11
Name some of the strategies in treating ARDS.

A11
The treatment revolves around maintaining good oxygenation and reducing tidal volumes. You must treat the underlying cause and provide supportive treatments including ventilation as required. Treatment must include careful fluid management.

Head Injuries

Q1
What are the main components of physical examination of a patient with a head injury?

A1
1. Assessment of airway, breathing and circulation (ABC)
2. Assessment of other major injuries: chest, abdomen, pelvis and spine
3. Examination of the scalp (lacerations and fractures)
4. Assessment of the face: cerebrospinal fluid (CSF), otorrhoea, CSF rhinorrhoea, haematotympanum and bilateral orbital ecchymoses are particularly looked for
5. Determination of Glasgow Coma Score (3–15)
6. Complete neurological examination: eye score, motor impairment, brain stem reflexes and signs of transtentorial herniation are carefully assessed

Q2
What signs suggest transtentorial herniation?

A2
1. Lethargy or progressive coma owing to depression of the reticular activating system
2. Asymmetric motor findings
3. Third nerve palsy (which may be bilateral)

Q3
What are the indications for computed tomography (CT) in head injury?

A3
Focal neurological symptoms and signs, reduced level of consciousness (e.g. Glasgow Coma Score < 12) and symptoms and signs of intracranial hypertension.

Q4
What is the value of normal intracranial pressure (ICP)?

A4
Approximately 10 mmHg.

Q5
How is ICP monitored?

A5
ICP can be monitored by introducing a fluid-filled catheter into the lateral ventricle.

Q6
Describe the intracranial compliance curve

A6
See Figure 2

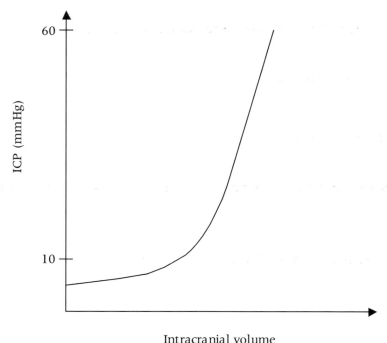

Figure 2

As the intracranial volume increases, there is at first a slow rise in ICP due to compensatory decrease in the volume of CSF and blood within the skull. If intracranial volume continues to rise, further compensation becomes impossible and the ICP increases rapidly causing intracranial hypertension (ICP > 20 mmHg).

Q7
What causes the rise in ICP following a severe head injury?

A7
The rise in ICP may be due to:
1. An intracranial haematoma
2. Cerebral oedema
3. Increased intracranial blood volume

Q8
Give two non-operative methods of reducing ICP

A8
1. Mechanical hyperventilation
2. Diuretics, e.g. mannitol (0.3–1.0 g/kg)

Q9
How would you specifically treat depressed skull fractures and compound skull fractures?

A9
1. Skull fractures depressed more than the thickness of the skull (> 5 mm) should be elevated. Depressed fractures overlying the dural sinuses should be left undisturbed unless surgery is indicated for a deteriorating condition
2. Compound fractures should be debrided and closed within 24 hours. Systemic antibiotics are also given

Q10
What are the main complications of depressed skull fractures?

A10
1. Meningitis
2. Intracranial abscess
3. Epilepsy (in 30% of cases)

Q11
What are the abnormal findings in the tomogram of the head shown in Figure 3?

A11
Left extradural haematoma and a slight shift of the midline to the contralateral side. Left-sided soft tissue swelling is also notable.

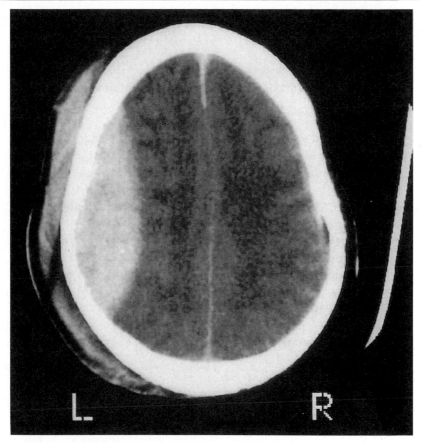

Figure 3

Q12
What are the criteria for hospital admission after head injury?

A12
1. History of loss of consciousness in a patient who has no responsible cancer
2. Neurological symptoms or signs
3. Skull fracture
4. Difficulty in assessing the patient, e.g. when under the influence of alcohol

5.   Glasgow Coma Score < 15

Sepsis

Q1
What are the features of the systemic inflammatory response syndrome(SIRS)?

A1
1. Temperature of < 36°C or > 38°C
2. Heart rate > 90 beats/min
3. Respiratory rate > 20/min
4. White blood count of < 4 or > 11

Q2
Define bacteraemia, septicaemia and sepsis.

A2
Bacteraemia is when bacteria are found in blood. Septicaemia is when bacteria are replicating in blood. Sepsis is when you have a documented source of infection and two or more of the features of the systemic inflammatory response syndrome.

Q3
Define severe sepsis and septic shock.

A3
Severe sepsis is when you have sepsis and altered organ perfusion/evidence of dysfunction of one or more organs. Septic shock is refractory hypotension with sepsis (i.e. in the presence of invasive infection).

Q4
What is the approximate mortality of a surgical patient with major sepsis/septic shock?

A4
This remains around 50%.

Nutrition

Q1
Describe the metabolic responses to fasting.

A1
There is a reduction in metabolic rate. Insulin levels fall and glucagon levels increase. There is hepatic glycogenolysis and gluconeogenesis. There is catabolism of muscle and visceral protein, and lipolysis. In addition there is an adaptive ketogenesis.

Q2
Describe the metabolic response to injury.

A2
In addition to a small rise in metabolic rate, there is a rise in hormone release (adrenaline, noradrenaline, glucagon, cortisol and growth hormone). The tissues show insulin resistance and there is a preference to use lipids as an energy source. Even with feeding there is increased gluconeogenesis and breakdown of muscle protein.

Q3
Describe the metabolic response to sepsis.

A3
There is a greater increase in metabolic rate with increasing energy requirements. Tissue resistance to insulin is common and can be severe. There is increased gluconeogenesis and protein catabolism with muscle wasting. Fluid retention is common.

Q4
Name four ways of assessing nutritional status.

A4
1. Clinical assessment, e.g. strength, appearance
2. Anthropometrically
3. Weight

4. Biochemically/haematologically, e.g. serum proteins

Q5
What is the approximate requirement for sodium and potassium in the healthy state?

A5
The approximate requirement is 1 mmol/kg/day of potassium and 2 mmol/kg/day of sodium.

Q6
What is the approximate energy and protein requirement in the healthy and septic states?

A6
The normal requirements are:
- Energy – approximately 1800–2000 kcal/day
- Protein – approximately 10 g of nitrogen/day

The septic patient requires:
- Energy – approximately 2500 kcal/day
- Protein – approximately 20 g of nitrogen/day

Q7
When might enteral nutrition be used?

A7
It can be used when oral intake is inadequate and treatment does not involve resting the gut. In addition, the proximal small bowel must be intact and functional.

Q8
What are some of the contra-indications to enteral nutrition?

A8
These include complete small bowel obstruction, severe diarrhoea, proximal small bowel fistula and severe pancreatitis.

Q9
List some of the complications of total parenteral nutrition.

A9
- Catheter related, e.g. infective
- Mechanical, e.g. thrombosis, migration
- Metabolic, e.g. hyperglycaemia/hypoglycaemia, raised tri-glycerides/cholesterol

Renal Failure

Q1
List three functions of the kidneys.

A1
1. Removal of the waste products of metabolism and some drugs
2. Endocrine
3. Regulating fluid/electrolyte homeostasis

Q2
What test can be useful in discriminating between acute renal failure and other causes of oliguria?

A2
Calculating the fractional excretion of sodium can be used. In acute renal failure, the ability of the tubules to resorb sodium is reduced, and therefore the fractional excretion of sodium rises to > 1%.

Q3
List three indications for renal replacement therapy in renal failure.

A3
1. Pulmonary oedema
2. Metabolic acidosis
3. Hyperkalaemia

SECTION 3

Pathology and Principles of Surgery

Abdominal Mass

Q1

A 75-year-old man presented with a painful throbbing abdominal mass. Investigations included computed tomography of the abdomen (Figure 4). What is the diagnosis?

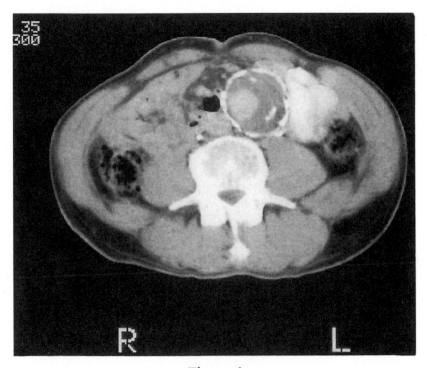

Figure 4

A1

The patient has an abdominal aortic aneurysm with evidence suggestive of previous aortic dissection (double calcification shadow in the aneurysm wall).

Q2

What are the indications for an aortogram?

A2
1.   Suspected suprarenal involvement
2.   Suggestion of mesenteric arterial insufficiency
3.   Suspected renovascular disease
4.   Ultrasound evidence of horseshoe or pelvic kidney
5.   Unexplained renal impairment

Q3
What are the indications for treatment of abdominal aortic aneurysm?

A3
1.   Surgery is mandatory for tender, symptomatic or rapidly enlarging aneurysms on serial ultrasound scans
2.   Surgery is recommended for all aneurysms equal to or greater than 5 cm in diameter
3.   Aneurysms less than 5 cm in diameter can also rupture (risk 20%) and may require treatment
4.   The risk of rupture should be compared with the risk of the surgery when considering surgery for asymptomatic aortic aneurysms

Q4
The same patient presented to the emergency room with severe abdominal pain radiating to the back. His blood pressure was 90/50 and the abdominal mass was tender on palpation. What is the diagnosis and how would you manage the case?

A4
The diagnosis is leaking (or ruptured) aortic aneurysm. I would perform a laparotomy as soon as intravenous fluids had been started and blood sent for crossmatching. I would control the aorta proximal to the aneurysm and repair the aneurysm using a Dacron graft. The laminated clot is removed and the outer wall is closed over the graft.

Q5
What is the survival rate for ruptured aortic aneurysm?

A5
Approximately 50%.

Q6
What is the commonest site for peripheral arterial aneurysms?

A6
The popliteal artery (accounts for 70% of cases).

Q7
How do popliteal aneurysms present?

A7
1. Ischaemia of the lower leg of acute onset due to thrombosis
2. Recurrent episodes of ischaemia and emolisation
3. A lump in the popliteal fossa
4. Symptoms related to compression of the popliteal vein or tibial nerve

Q8
What are the indications for treatment of popliteal aneurysms?

A8
1. Pregangrenous ischaemia due to acute thrombosis (requires immediate surgery)
2. Recurrent peripheral embolisation (requires early surgery)
3. Asymptomatic aneurysm if the external diameter is more than three times the normal arterial diameter of the popliteal artery

Q9
What are the principles of surgical treatment of popliteal aneurysms?

A9
1. Resection of the aneurysm and graft replacement or
2. Exclusion of aneurysm and bypass with saphenous vein grafts

Q10
Describe the main histopathological features of atherosclerotic abdominal aortic aneurysms

A10
1. Intimal atheroma
2. Ischaemia and fibrosis
3. Loss of elastic tissue owing to degradation by proteolytic enzymes such as metalloproteinases
4. Inflammatory cells, including macrophages, infiltrating the arterial wall. These release various cytokines, which mediate the inflammatory effects

Thrombosis and Embolism

Q1
What is a *thrombus* and what are the predisposing factors?

A1
A thrombus is a solid mass of blood constituents that has formed within the vascular system. The predisposing factors (Virchow's triad) are:
- Abnormalities of the vessel wall
- Abnormalities of blood flow
- Abnormalities of blood constituents

Arterial thrombosis is most commonly over an atheromatous plaque. Venous thrombosis is most commonly due to stasis.

Q2
What is an *embolus* and what do they usually consist of?

A2
An embolus is a mass of material in the vascular system that is able to lodge within a vessel and block its lumen. Types of embolic material include thrombi (most emboli), tumour fragments, amniotic fluid, gas, fat, atheromatous plaque material and heart-valve vegetations. They most commonly occur as pulmonary emboli from deep-leg vein thrombosis.

Q3
Define *infarction* and *gangrene*.

A3
Infarction is the ischaemic death of tissues. Gangrene is infarction of a mixture of tissues in bulk, e.g. part of a limb.

Amyloid

Q1
What is *amyloid* and how is amyloidosis classified?

A1
Amyloid is the name given to proteins/glycoproteins that share the following properties:
- B-pleated sheet structure
- Tendency to cause tissues to become hardened and waxy
- Have an extracellular location (often on the basement membranes)

Amyloid can be classified according to aetiology, tissue distribution and chemical composition. It can either be systemic or localised.

Q2
How can systemic amyloid be further classified?

A2
Further classification can be made according to aetiology. These include:
- Myeloma associated – amyloid substance AL (immunoglobulin light chains/fragments)
- Reactive – amyloid substance AA (serum amyloid protein A)
- Senile – amyloid substance AS (prealbumin)
- Haemodialysis associated – amyloid substance AH (B2-microglobulin)

Q3
List some of the clinical manifestations of amyloidosis.

A3
These include cardiac failure secondary to restrictive cardiomyopathy, nephrotic syndrome, carpal tunnel syndrome, hepatosplenomegaly and macroglossia.

Breast Cancer

Q1
What physical signs suggest that a breast lump may be malignant?

A1
1. Hard lump
2. Poorly defined margins
3. Skin tethering
4. Fixation to underlying structures
5. Palpable axillary nodes
6. Nipple retraction
7. Skin ulceration

Q2
How would you investigate a suspicious lump in the breast?

A2
I would perform the following investigations:

1. Mammography
2. Fine-needle aspiration cytology or core biopsy
3. Ultrasound determines whether a lump is solid or cystic. The addition of Doppler imaging determines the vascularity of the lump (highly vascular lumps are more likely to be malignant)
4. Excisional or incisional biopsy may be required
5. If there is suspicion of metastatic disease, screening tests such as liver ultrasonography, bone scan and chest radiography may be carried out.

Q3
How would you treat a 54-year-old woman with a 2 cm malignant lump in the outer quadrant of the breast with no evidence of regional or distant metastases?

A3

1. I would perform a wide local excision (or quadrantectomy) of the lump removing a 1.5 cm margin of healthy tissue down to the pectoral fascia. The excision is combined with axillary dissection
2. The patient is prescribed tamoxifen 20 mg daily for 5 years
3. The patient is treated with radiotherapy to the whole breast with a booster to the tumour bed
4. If the tumour is poorly differentiated or the axillary nodes are involved, the patient should be considered for chemotherapy such as CMF (cyclophosphamide, methotrexate and fluorouracil) regimen

Q4

What are the objectives of axillary dissection?

A4

1. Determination of progress
2. Assessment of the need for systemic chemotherapy
3. Reduction of the incidence of axillary recurrence. It has no impact on survival

Q5

What does DCIS refer to?

A5

Ductal carcinoma *in situ* refers to proliferation of ductal epithelial cells identical in morphology to invasive carcinoma cells without breaching the basement membrane.

Q6

What are the principles of DCIS treatment?

A6

DCIS can be adequately treated by wide local excision (1 cm of normal tissue margin) and postoperative radiotherapy. Extensive and multifocal DCIS is treated by mastectomy. Adjuvant tamoxifen therapy is being assessed in clinical trials.

Q7

Is axillary dissection required for DCIS?

A7
No. The incidence of axillary metastases is less than 1%.

Q8
What are the main histopathological types of DCIS?

A8
DCIS can be classified into three types:

- High nuclear grade (HNG)
- Intermediate nuclear grade
- Low nuclear grade (LNG)

Most comedo-type lesions are HNG DCIS. The LNG lesions include papillary and cribriform subtypes. The presence of necrosis is a poor prognostic indicator.

Q9
Is there a difference in management between HNG and LNG types of DCIS?

A9
Yes. HNG lesions are associated with a higher incidence of local recurrence, therefore postoperative radiotherapy is required if conservative surgery is performed. LNG lesions can be treated with adequate local excision only. The presence of necrosis and lesion size also influence treatment decisions.

Q10
What are the principles of postoperative adjuvant systemic therapy in patients with invasive breast cancer?

A10
1. All patients with oestrogen receptor positive (ER+) tumours are prescribed tamoxifen (20 mg daily for 2–5 years)
2. Postoperative chemotherapy is indicated in fit patients with:

- Poorly differentiated tumours
- Positive axillary nodes
- Large primary tumours
- Widespread disease
- Oestrogen receptor negative (ER–) tumours
3. Leuteinising hormone releasing hormone (LHRH) agonists may be considered in premenopausal women with advanced breast cancer

Various chemotherapy regimens are available. Recently paclitaxel has been introduced.

Q11
Consider the craniocaudal mammogram of the left breast in Figure 5. What does it show?

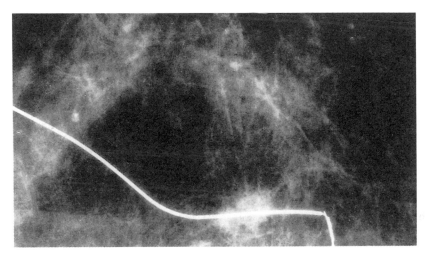

Figure 5

A11
It shows a localisation wire marking a well defined lesion with a stellate periphery very suggestive of carcinoma. The lesion is located deep in the breast and just lateral to the midline.

Q12

Is it possible to confirm the diagnosis of carcinoma before operation in this case (there is no palpable lump)?

A12

Yes. Stereotactic core biopsy allows a preoperative histological diagnosis.

Q13

What impact has stereotactic core biopsy had on breast cancer screening?

A13

It has altered decisions beneficially in approximately 65% of cases. The numbers of benign localisation biopsies and the number of clinical follow-ups have been significantly reduced with stereotactic core biopsy.

Q14

What is meant by a 'sentinel node'?

A14

This is the first lymph node to drain the primary tumour.

Q15

How is the sentinel node identified during axillary dissection?

A15

It can be identified using a vital blue dye and/or a radioactive-isotope-labelled albumin solution injected before the operation. In the radioisotope technique intraoperative identification is facilitated by the use of a hand-held gamma probe.

Bowel Obstruction

Q1
How would you manage an 80-year-old man who is referred to you by the Accident and Emergency Department with abdominal pain, distension and vomiting?

A1
1. A detailed history is obtained
2. A thorough and complete clinical examination is performed
   - Pyrexia and abdominal tenderness are looked for, as they may indicate bowel strangulation
   - Hernial orifices are examined
   - Degree of dehydration is determined. Skin turgor, blood pressure, pulse and jugular vein pressure (JVP) are useful parameters for assessing hypovolaemia
3. A venous access is obtained, which may be a peripheral cannula or a central line in grossly dehydrated patients, and intravenous fluids are started
4. Blood tests are carried out
   - Full blood count (white cell count may indicate bowel strangulation)
   - Serum urea, creatinine and electrolytes
   - Serum amylase and glucose
5. A urinary catheter is inserted in very ill and severely dehydrated patients
6. A plain abdominal radiograph and an erect chest radiograph are obtained
7. A nasogastric tube is inserted
8. A decision is made as to whether the patient is to be managed conservatively or operatively

Q2
What are the indications for urgent operative management in a patient with small bowel obstruction?

A2
Bowel strangulation, as suggested by pyrexia, abdominal tenderness, leukocytosis and/or the presence of irreducible hernia.

Q3
Describe the procedure of insertion of a central venous catheter into the internal jugular vein

A3
1. The procedure is explained to the patient
2. The patient is positioned supine with 25° head-down tilt. The face is turned to the contralateral side (usually to the left)
3. The skin is prepared with an antiseptic (e.g. chlorhexidine)
4. A local anaesthetic (e.g. 1% or 2% lignocaine) is infiltrated into the skin midway between the earlobe and the sternal end of the clavicle (at the site of the carotid pulsation)
5. The fingers of the left hand are used to displace the carotid artery medially, while the cannula is inserted into the internal jugular vein using the right hand. The cannula should enter the skin at 35° aiming at the sternal end of the clavicle. A 'give' is felt when the cannula enters the deep fascia and another when it enters the vein. Reflux of venous blood confirms venous cannulation. The needle is then withdrawn and a guide wire is passed through the cannula. The latter is withdrawn and a catheter is passed over the guide wire so that its tip lies in the right atrium. The catheter is then fixed to the skin with silk sutures and its entry point is covered with Opsite.
6. A plain chest radiograph is taken to confirm the correct position of the catheter

Q4
What is the normal central venous pressure (CVP)?

A4
The normal CVP is 2–8 cmH$_2$O.

Q5
What are the principles of surgical treatment in a 70-year-old man with obstructive sigmoid carcinoma?

A5

1. Fluid resuscitation and informed consent for laparotomy and colostomy
2. Laparotomy through a midline incision
3. Excision of the colonic segment containing the lesion with adequate margins. The excision includes the mesocolon containing the lymph nodes draining the area
4. An end colostomy (proximal colon) is fashioned if primary anastomosis is not safe due to dilatation, lack of bowel preparation and/or the patient's poor health. In such cases the distal end is closed or brought to the surface as a mucous fistula. Alternatively a primary anastomosis is performed after on-table colonic lavage or subtotal colectomy and ileocolic anastomosis.

Q6

What is the commonest cause of large bowel obstruction in the UK?

A6

Colorectal carcinoma.

Q7

Consider the plain abdominal radiograph in Figure 6. What is the most likely diagnosis in this patient?

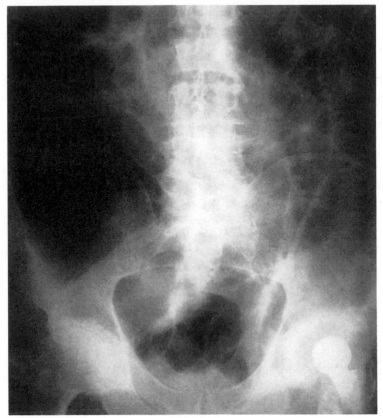

Figure 6

A7

The plain radiograph reveals dilatation of small and large bowel suggestive of large bowel obstruction with an incompetent ileocaecal valve. The shadow at the left inguinal region raises the possibility of a strangulated inguinal hernia. A left total hip arthroplasty is also shown.

The Acute Abdomen

Q1

A 57-year-old patient presents with sudden onset of severe epigastric pain radiating to the right shoulder. What are the top three differential diagnoses?

A1

1. Perforated peptic ulcer
2. Acute pancreatitis
3. Acute cholecystitis

Q2

An erect radiograph (Figure 7) was obtained in the emergency room. What is the most likely diagnosis?

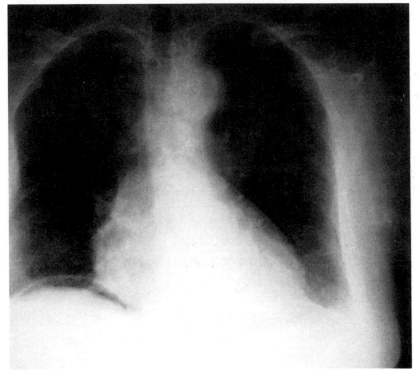

Figure 7

A2
The radiograph shows free gas under the hemidiaphragms – a perforated peptic ulcer is the most likely diagnosis.

Q3
Does the absence of free gas under the hemidiaphragm exclude the diagnosis?

A3
No. Subdiaphragmatic gas is seen in approximately 85% of plain chest radiographs.

Q4

How would you manage this patient?

A4

1. A nasogastric tube is inserted
2. Blood is obtained and sent for laboratory analysis including crossmatching
3. Intravenous fluids are commenced
4. Intravenous broad-spectrum antimicrobials are commenced (e.g. cefuroxime, cefazolin, cefoxitin)
5. The patient undergoes laparatomy, peritoneal lavage and simple closure of the hole using an omental patch and absorbable sutures. A definitive ulcer operation may be performed if indicated, e.g. truncal vagotomy and pyloroplasty or highly selective vagotomy. Alternatively, laparoscopic repair of the perforation may be possible. The hole is again covered with a suitable omental patch, which is fixed *in situ* using endoscopic clips

Q5

If a peptic ulcer biopsy demonstrates *Helicobacter pylori*-like organisms (HLOs), how can this be eradicated?

A5

H. pylori can be eradicated by a course of triple therapy, e.g. a 1 week course of amoxycillin (1 g twice daily), metronidazole (400 mg twice daily) and lansoprazole (30 mg twice daily).

Transplantation

Q1
Give a brief account of the three main types of allograft rejection

A1
1. Hyperacute rejection occurs when the serum of the recipient has preformed antibodies against the donor antigens. These antibodies adhere to the endothelium of the graft causing thrombosis and graft infarction within hours of transplantation. This type of rejection is treated by graft removal
2. Acute rejection is a cell-mediated process involving CD4 immunocytes. It usually presents within 3 months of transplantation and causes graft dysfunction. The diagnosis can be confirmed with biopsy. It is treated with corticosteroids
3. Chronic rejection usually occurs more than a year after transplant. It involves humoral and cell-mediated immune responses. It is not treatable or reversible

Q2
What is meant by HLA matching? Is HLA matching important in liver transplantation?

A2
Human leukocyte antigens are histocompatibility antigens and are defined by tissue typing. The six human genes (A, B, C, DP, DQ, DR) are located on chromosome 6. HLA-C, HLA-DP and HLA-DQ do not seem to be important in transplantation. HLA matching at A, B and DR loci is important for renal and/or pancreatic transplantation. It is not important in cardiac and hepatic transplantation. ABO blood groups must be identical or compatible in renal, hepatic, cardiac and pancreatic transplants.

Q3
What are the operative principles of renal transplantation in adults?

A3

1. The donor kidney is implanted in the contralateral iliac fossa (heterotopic transplantation).
2. The donor renal vein is anastomosed to the external iliac vein (end-to-side anastomosis)
3. The donor renal artery is anastomosed to the external iliac artery (end-to-side anastomosis)
4. The ureter is anastomosed to the dome of the bladder with sub-mucosal tunnelling to prevent reflux

Q4

Outline the operative principles of orthotopic liver transplantation (OLT)

A4

1. A bilateral subcostal incision with upward extension to the xiphoid process is made
2. The suprahepatic and infrahepatic vena caval anastomoses are made
3. The donor and recipient portal veins are anastomosed end to end
4. The donor and recipient common hepatic arteries are anastomosed end to end
5. The donor and recipient common bile ducts (CBDs) are anastomosed end to end. Alternatively a choledochojejunostomy (Roux-en-Y) is performed if there is no recipient CBD
6. The donor gall bladder is removed and a liver biopsy is performed

Q5

What is the 5 year graft survival rate for renal transplants?

A5

It is 80% for living related donor kidneys and 67% for cadaveric donor kidneys.

Q6

Outline the criteria for the diagnosis of brain-stem death in the UK

A6

1. The patient is in apnoeic coma
2. Abnormal plasma electrolytes and blood gases, drug intoxication and hypothermia are the exclusion criteria
3. There is an absence of brainstem reflexes, including papillary, corneal, vestibulo-ocular, oculocephalic and gag reflexes
4. The diagnosis is made by two independent medical practitioners on two separate occasions. Neither doctor should be part of the transplant team.

Replacement Arthroplasty

Q1
What are the features of an ideal replacement arthroplasty?

A1
1. It provides a good range of movement
2. It has a low coefficient of friction
3. It has a low rate of wear
4. It is tissue compatible
5. It is revisable in component failure
6. It has adequate mechanical strength
7. It provides complete pain relief
8. It has mechanical stability

Q2
Name some materials used for manufacturing a hip joint prosthesis

A2
1. Ultra-high-molecular-weight polyethylene
2. Titanium
3. Cobalt–chrome alloys

Q3
What are the main complications of replacement arthroplasty?

A3
1. Infection
2. Component failure
3. Dislocation
4. Mechanical loosening
5. Metal sensitivity
6. Haematoma, deep vein thrombosis, pulmonary embolism, urinary tract infection, pressure sores, neurovascular injury, confusion, myocardial infarction, etc.

Q4

What factors can reduce the incidence of infection?

A4
1. Use of perioperative systemic antimicrobials
2. Use of antimicrobial-loaded cement
3. Laminant airflow ventilation in the operating rooms
4. Thorough scrubbing, disposable gowns, changing gloves and good skin preparation
5. Gentle handling of tissues, adequate haemostasis and good suturing techniques
6. Optimisation of tissue oxygenation

Q5
What techniques are known to reduce the incidence of mechanical loosening?

A5
1. Use of a dry operative field
2. Introduction of cement under pressure
3. Lavage systems
4. Cement restrictions

SECTION 4

Miscellaneous Topics

Controlled Clinical Trials

Q1
What is meant by 'controlled clinical trials'?

A1
A controlled trial is an experiment in which one or more treatments are compared with a control treatment, which can be nothing, a placebo or a standard clinical practice. A controlled trial is necessary when experience alone does not provide sufficient evidence for selecting the best course of clinical action.

Q2
What does a clinical trial protocol contain?

A2
1. An introduction, which includes the main references related to the study background
2. The aims of the study
3. A precise formulation of the questions
4. Material (populations, number of patients)
5. Randomisation method
6. Methods (end point, who will perform the evaluation and at what time)
7. Results
8. Statistical methods
9. Ethical aspects (ethical approval, consent forms)
10. Start and completion dates
11. Bibliography
12. Presentation of results
13. Proposed publication
14. Financial support
15. Responsibilities of the various workers
16. Signatures from all co-workers

Q3
What is the power of the trial?

A3

The power of the trial measures the sensitivity of the trial to detect an actual difference and equals type II error (β).

Q4

What statistical factors does the number of patients required for a clinical trial depend on?

A4

1. Type I error (2α)
2. Type II error (β)
3. Minimal relevant difference (Δ)

Q5

What is meant by crossover designs for clinical trials?

A5

In crossover designs the patient acts as his or her own control. Several treatments can be compared, the order of which should be random. Treatments intended to relieve chronic symptoms are particularly suitable.

Q6

What is meant by randomisation?

A6

Randomisation is a method of assignment of subjects to either experimental or control treatments whereby each patient has an equal chance of appearing in any treatment group. It protects against selection bias and allows control of other clinical variables that may affect the outcomes under investigation.

Q7

When is the double-blinding technique most desirable?

A7

When the end points in the trial are subjective, e.g. improved/un-changed/worse.

Medical Statistics

Q1
In medical statistics, what is meant by type I and type II errors?

A1
Type I error occurs when, as a result of statistical testing, the null hypothesis (H_0) is rejected when it is true (i.e. ought not to be rejected). Type II error is the error when, as a result of statistical testing, the null hypothesis is not rejected when it is false (i.e. it should have been rejected).

Q2
If you are investigating an association between the intake of non-steroidal anti-inflammatory drugs (NSAIDs) and the incidence of colorectal cancer, what does the null hypothesis state?

A2
H_0 states that there is no difference in NSAID intake between G1 patients (with a history of colorectal cancer) and G2 hospital patients (without a history of colorectal cancer)

Q3
What does 'level of significance' refer to?

A3
It refers to the statistical probability related to type I error.

Q4
Define sensitivity and specificity

A4
Sensitivity refers to the ability to identify (correctly) the people who have the condition under investigation. Specificity refers to the ability to identify (correctly) those who do not have the condition under investigation.

$$\text{Sensitivity} = \frac{\text{Number tested as positive}}{\text{Total with the condition}}$$

$$\text{Specificity} = \frac{\text{Number tested as negative}}{\text{Total without the condition}}$$

Q5
If you have data which is skewed in distribution, how would you calculate a standard distribution?

A5
Firstly I would transform the data into normal distribution using log or ln, and secondly I would calculate the standard deviation (which measures the scatter of the normalised data around the mean) as follows:

$$\text{SD} = \frac{\sum (x - \bar{x})^2}{n-1}$$

Q6
What does 'confidence interval' mean?

A6
Confidence intervals give the probability of a true population mean lying within a range derived from a sample mean and its standard error. For example, there is a 95% probability that the true population mean lies within

$$\text{Sample mean} \pm (1.96 \times \text{standard error of the mean})$$

Q7
What is Student's *t*-test?

A7
It is a parametric test based on the *t*-distribution and is used for comparing a single small sample with a population or to compare the difference in

means between two small samples. It is inappropriate if more than two means are compared.

Q8
What does the *t*-distribution look like?

A8
It is identical to the normal distribution at infinite degrees of freedom.

Q9
What statistical test would you use (1) to compare the means for three independent groups and (2) to test the significance of the relationship between two variables that are cross-tabulated in a contingency table?

A9
1. Analysis of variance is the most appropriate
2. The chi-squared test is the most appropriate

Q10
What is the difference between linear regression and correlation?

A10
Linear regression is a technique used to analyse relationships between variables. Regression analysis can be used to identify the straight line that runs through data points with the best possible fit. Correlation indicates the nature and strength of the relationship between the two variables.

Surgical Audit/Informed Consent

Q1
What is meant by 'surgical audit'?

A1
Surgical audit is the critical and systematic analysis of quality of surgical care, the aim of which is to improve the standards of surgical care. Most audits are retrospective studies.

Q2
What are the main subtypes of surgical audit?

A2
1. Audit of structure. This refers to the organisation and availability of resources to deliver the surgical service
2. Audit of process. This refers to the way the patient has been managed from admission to discharge
3. Audit of outcome. This is the audit of surgical intervention

Q3
What are the stages of a single audit?

A3
1. Primary data collection. This is best performed by junior doctors or an audit officer. Specific audit forms are widely used. Computers are particularly useful
2. Verification of primary data through confidential peer review
3. Submission of data to analysis
4. Audit meetings should be held regularly, e.g. fortnightly, and should be attended by all members of the surgical team including representatives of the nursing staff

Q4
What characteristics make a surgical audit successful?

A4
A successful audit is:

1. Complete
2. Honest
3. Accurate
4. Educational
5. Confidential
6. Objective
7. Reproducible
8. Cost effective

Q5
How do you quantify the quality of life and satisfaction of the patient?

A5
This can be evaluated using a system of QALYs (quality adjusted life years). One year of current life in perfect health is 1 QALY and one year at a lower level is 1 q.

Q6
Does audit have limitations that you can perceive?

A6
Yes, many limitations exist:

1. Comparison of an individual's results with published results is extremely difficult
2. Accurate assessment of the patient's quality of life is difficult
3. Surgeons may select cases to affect the outcome
4. Alternative treatments or the no-treatment options are not assessed

Q7
What is meant by 'informed consent'?

A7
Informed consent means that the procedure is carefully explained to the patient in a balanced and unemotional way stating all significant risks

associated with the procedure and explaining alternative treatments. The patient has a legal right to withhold consent and there is nothing the doctor can do about it provided the patient has a sound mind.

Q8
Who gives consent in the following situations in the UK:
(1)   A 15-year-old requiring an orchidopexy
(2)   A 63-year-old who is unconscious and requires an emergency operation

A8
1.   Children under 16 years of age are legally unable to give consent, and the parent or guardian gives consent on their behalf. The procedure and its potential risks are explained to the child and the parent or guardian.
2.   In the case of an unconscious patient, the next of kin can give consent. If no next of kin is available, it is wise to obtain a colleague's agreement with the surgical procedure proposed, written in the notes. The law recognises that it is in the patient's best interest for such an emergency treatment to go ahead.

Screening

Q1
What is meant by screening?

A1
Screening is a process aimed at the presumptive identification of unrecognised disease using procedures that can be applied rapidly and economically to a certain population. Screening tests are not usually diagnostic, and further tests and examinations are required to establish the diagnosis.

Q2
What are the requirements for a screening programme?

A2
1. High prevalence of the condition to be screened
2. A condition sufficiently serious to justify the effort and cost
3. Possibility of detecting the disease at a stage at which treatment is easier and more effective than when the disease declares itself in the usual manner
4. Availability of a screening test that is simple, inexpensive and acceptable to the people screened
5. An acceptable level of false positives and false negatives

Q3
What are the main characteristics of the screening test?

A3
1. Validity, measured by sensitivity and specificity
2. Predictive value, which is the percentage of false positives and false negatives
3. Replicability

Q4
When screening for colorectal cancer, which patients are regarded as at high risk?

A4
Patients with:

1. Long-standing ulcerative colitis
2. Familial polyposis coli
3. Muir syndrome
4. Lynch syndrome
5. Ureterosigmoidostomy
6. Crohn's colitis
7. Turcot's syndrome
8. Gardner's syndrome
9. Peutz–Jeghers' syndrome
10. Family cancer syndrome
11. History of colorectal cancer

Q5
What are the main methods of screening in colorectal cancer?

A5
1. Digital rectal examination
2. Proctosigmoidoscopy (rigid or flexible)
3. Colonoscopy
4. Barium enema
5. Faecal occult blood testing
6. Serum tumour markers

Q6
What are the main tests for faecal occult blood detection?

A6
1. Haemoccult
2. Hemo quant
3. Immunological methods

Q7
Which cancer markers can be used in colorectal cancer screening?

A7
1. Carcinoembryonic antigen

2. DNA flow cytometry of colonic biopsies
3. Faecal lithocholic/deoxycholic acid ratio
4. Monosialganglioside antigen

Q8
What is the genetic basis for familial polyposis coli?

A8
Autosomal dominant inheritance. The gene is located on chromosome 5.

Q9
What are the principles of screening for breast cancer?

A9
1. All women over the age of 50 years are advised to have a mammogram every 1–3 years
2. There is a growing body of opinion that mammographic screening is effective in women aged 40–50 years
3. Patients with mammographic abnormalities are referred to a breast specialist for clinical examination and further investigations

Q10
Has breast cancer screening been shown to reduce mortality rates?

A10
Yes, by approximately 30% in women over the age of 50.

Q11
What are the main features of breast cancer detected by screening?

A11
It is:

1. More likely to be carcinoma *in situ*
2. Associated with a smaller incidence of axillary node involvement

3.   Smaller
4.   More likely to be well differentiated

Q12
What percentage of breast cancers are familial and what is the genetic basis?

A12
Approximately 5% of all breast cancers are familial.

At least fives genes are responsible. The *BRCA1* gene (on chromosome 17) has been cloned in the USA. It accounts for approximately 40% of familial breast cancers. Other genes include *BRCA2* (on chromosome 13), *p53* (on chromosome 17) and the ataxia telangiectasia gene.